L.F.C.
PREMIER LEAGUE
CHAMPONS
2019-20

Designed by **Daniel May**

g

A Grange Publication

© 2020. Published by Grange Communications Ltd., Edinburgh, under licence from The Liverpool Football Club and Athletic Grounds Ltd. Printed in the EU.

Photographs © Liverpool FC and AG Ltd., PA Images

Special thanks to Matic Marin for the illustration on p.94-95

ISBN 978-1-913578-20-6

CONTENTS

FROM DOUBTERS
TO BELIEVERS

Thursday 25 June 2020 is a date that will forever be etched in the annals of LFC history. For it was on this night that Liverpool's lengthy wait to become Premier League champions finally came to a glorious conclusion.

This magical, long-craved moment arrived shortly after 10pm in West London, when the final whistle blew at Stamford Bridge. The Reds weren't actively involved, they'd comprehensively beaten Crystal Palace 4-0 the night before, but Manchester City's 2-1 defeat to Chelsea, meant the season-long leaders could no longer be caught at the top.

It was the cue for a mass outpouring of emotion and celebration; relief and elation being the overriding feelings of Liverpudlians worldwide. During a three-decade spell in which every other trophy had been brought back to Anfield, this was the one that had so frustratingly eluded Liverpool's clutches.

After the previous season's near miss – when the Reds finished second despite losing only one game – not to mention the anguish of getting so close in 2014, it truly was a moment to savour.

From day one of the 2019/20 campaign, Jürgen Klopp's team looked determined to go one better and the pace at which they burst off the starting blocks left everyone trailing in their wake.

The impressive style shown during a long unbeaten run left football writers searching for new superlatives. Some teams were swatted aside with ease, other games required more resilience. What was always evident though was this side's relentless will to win.

It wasn't until the last day of February that Liverpool first tasted defeat in the league, but by that stage of the season they were so far ahead of the chasing pack it didn't really matter.

The question now was when they would clinch the title, not if. It should have been sometime in March but the Covid-19 Pandemic brought everyday life as we knew it to a shuddering halt.

Thankfully, football eventually resumed and Liverpool were free to complete what had long been deemed inevitable. They were confirmed as champions for a 19th time with seven games to spare – the earliest an English top-flight title had ever been secured – and no one could deny that it wasn't fully deserved.

To see the trophy finally presented a few weeks later – a sight some supporters had feared they would never experience again – was the stuff dreams are made of.

Liverpool Football Club is once again officially the top team in England and this is the story of how an unforgettable league season unfolded.

FEELING CHAMPION

Jürgen Klopp and Jordan Henderson discuss Liverpool Football Club's 2019/20 Premier League title success from a manager and captain's perspective…

Being crowned champions of England

JK: It feels brilliant. The whole ride is a wonderful experience. It was very special. After the 97 points ride last year plus extension with the Champions League, and this season, and all the years before chasing the Champions League spot, I was thinking I want it as early as possible. I couldn't feel better. It's just a big relief and it feels like freedom, whatever, I don't know exactly. It's good.

JH: It has been an incredible year, really. What we have achieved as a team has been unbelievable and to top it off with the Premier League was really special for the lads, but also for the fans and the club. To lift that trophy is something that we've waited for, for a long time.

The unique togetherness within this squad

JH: A lot of it comes down to the manager. That was something he drove for when he first came. The togetherness of the players - not only on the pitch - off the pitch, you get to see people in a different light, more comfortable, you find out different things and just become closer to them. Off the pitch was really important: we've done stuff together in the past that has helped that bond and when you're winning games that helps as well. That togetherness has grown and it's at a point now where it's really strong. There are so many leaders within the dressing room, so many fantastic players that want to improve and want to be better. I think we just need to keep this squad of players together as long as possible and hopefully in the near future we can be more successful.

JK: These individuals make a team. It is about individuals and we can't underestimate how influential they all are. If you would give me now a list of five million players, I would love to pick these 25, 30 boys and say I want to do it with them. Because they are so incredibly close, because they understand how important it is to be self-confident on a high, high level but not overly confident that you think you are more important

> ## "These individuals make a team. It is about individuals and we can't underestimate how influential they all are."
>
> Jürgen Klopp

than others. Because without the others, we are nothing – absolutely. This game shows that every day and what I love so much about this game is that it keeps us humble. This game keeps us humble and helps us understand life in the best way.

Winning this title for the club, the city and its people

JK: It's just great to do it for these people because you know how much it means to them. These

years where I can be a part of this amazing football club and help bring success.

On what the future holds for this team

JK: We will stay greedy, we have to and we will. But if that then leads automatically to more trophies, I don't know because other teams have other reasons to make the next step. We will not change our attitude, we try to improve the attitude, we try to improve everything. Is it possible to do it for a longer period? Yes – I would say there's no reason,

> ## "It has been an incredible year, really. What we have achieved as a team has been unbelievable and to top it off with the Premier League was really special for the lads, but also for the fans and the club."
>
> Jordan Henderson

people deserve it so much. I think, success in football lifts the mood of the city always and I hope we can use that for the better for all parts which are necessary for this city.

JH: I feel as though Liverpool has been a part of my life for so long. My kids were born here, so it's always going to be a big part of my life. It is nice to win trophies and be a part of it, hopefully there's more to come in the future. It's such a special club, a unique club and I'm so lucky, honoured and humbled to have been a part of it for so long. I hope there's many more

there's absolutely no reason for it.

JH: I saw something that Kenny's [Dalglish] son posted on social media, when they won the trophy when he was a kid and he said he would never have thought it would have gone 30 years until they won a next one. That's why you've got to enjoy it, you never know what can happen in football. That's why you do need to keep the standards, stay hungry and play like a team that hasn't won anything before. If you do that, then I'm sure the Premier League trophy can be at Anfield many more times in the future.

Friday 9 August 2019 • Venue: Anfield • Attendance: 53,333 • Referee: Michael Oliver

LIVERPOOL 4 1 NORWICH CITY

Hanley OG (7) Van Dijk (28)
Salah (19) Origi (42)

Pukki (64)

MATCH OVERVIEW

Liverpool opened the season in style by racing into a four-goal lead before half-time against the newly promoted Canaries. Despite losing Alisson to a first half injury they went on to comfortably claim all three points.

THE TEAMS

Liverpool		Norwich City
Robertson		Aarons
van Dijk	Henderson c	Origi 85'	Buendía	McLean	Hanley c
Alisson 39'	Wijnaldum	Firmino 85'	Pukki 83'	Stiepermann 58'	Trybull 70'	Godfrey	Krul
Gomez	Fabinho	Salah		Cantwell	Lewis
Alexander-Arnold		

Used subs **Adrián** 39' ⬆ **Milner** 85' ⬆ **Mané** 85' ⬆

Used subs **Hernandez** 70' ⬆ **Leitner** 58' ⬆ **Drmic** 83' ⬆

"For 60 minutes we looked very sharp, then we have to control the game a bit more. Norwich have all my respect - they stayed cheeky, they enjoyed their football. At the start of the second half we could have scored a fifth or sixth goal, then Norwich scored. After that we were never in danger but had to work hard to keep the score what it was."

Jürgen Klopp

"It was the start of the Premier League, we wanted to go out and start really well, which we managed to do. We scored some brilliant goals and played well in the first half. In the second half we created some chances, but could have controlled the game a little bit better. There's still improvement [to be made] but overall we're delighted with the result and performance."

Jordan Henderson

Saturday 17 August 2019 • Venue: St Mary's • Attendance: 31,712 • Referee: Andre Marriner

SOUTHAMPTON 1 2 LIVERPOOL

Ings (83)

Mané (45)
Firmino (71)

MATCH OVERVIEW

From being in a position where they looked to be cruising to victory, Liverpool failed to build on a 2-0 lead and had to endure a nervous end to this game but thankfully held on to run out winners.

THE TEAMS

Southampton

Gunn

Vestergaard
Yoshida
Bednarek

Bertrand 77'
Højbjerg c
Romeu 64'
Ward-Prowse
Valery

Redmond
Adams 68'

Liverpool

Alexander-Arnold
Matip
van Dijk
Robertson

Salah 79'
Oxlade-Chamberlain 89'
Firmino
Wijnaldum
Mané
Milner c 74'

Adrián

Used subs Ings 64' Djenepo 77' Armstrong 68'

Used subs Fabinho 74' Henderson 89' Origi 79'

"It was my first league start in a long time and it was just nice to be back out there. I remember sort of trying to feel my way into the game and I think I grew into it as the game went on. Ultimately it was a good win for us on the day."

Alex Oxlade-Chamberlain

"We controlled the game, we were fluent, all that stuff. Sadio scored a fantastic goal in pretty much the best moment of the first half. In the second half we… did a lot of good things, and then the boys felt the tiredness. [But] we kept the result, I think we deserved the three points… The boys did an outstanding job. Let's go home, recover and start again."

Jürgen Klopp

Saturday 24 August 2019 • Venue: Anfield • Attendance: 53,298 • Referee: Anthony Taylor

LIVERPOOL 3 1 ARSENAL

Matip (41)
Salah (49, 58)

Torreira (85)

MATCH OVERVIEW

Both teams went into this game with a one hundred per cent record from their opening two games but the gulf in class was clear to see as Liverpool moved up a gear to record a comprehensive victory.

THE TEAMS

LIVERPOOL

Robertson
van Dijk
Adrián 39'
Matip
Alexander-Arnold
Wijnaldum 69'
Fabinho
Henderson c
Mané 77'
Firmino 86'
Salah

ARSENAL

Maitland-Niles
Guendouzi 86'
Sokratis
Leno
Luiz
Monreal
Pépé
Ceballos 61'
Xhaka c
Willock 81'
Aubameyang

Used subs **Milner** 69' **Oxlade-Chamberlain** 77' **Lallana** 86'

Used subs **Torreira** 61' **Lacazette** 81' **Mkhitaryan** 86'

"I loved the desire, the passion, the power and the energy that we put into this game. It made us really uncomfortable to play against, which is what we wanted. We could have controlled it better, that's probably our real challenge…We are not Disneyland, we do not need to excite everyone in every second."

Jürgen Klopp

"We need to improve in possession and countering the pressure but Liverpool is the best team with this. We have to be realistic but we can fight closer to them."

Unai Emery (Arsenal manager)

Saturday 31 August 2019 • Venue: Turf Moor • Attendance: 21,762 • Referee: Chris Kavanagh

BURNLEY 0 3 LIVERPOOL

Wood OG (33)   Firmino (80)
Mané (37)

MATCH OVERVIEW

Once the deadlock was broken, Liverpool were never in any real danger of squandering the points. A first clean-sheet of the season was recorded and so too was a new club record 13th consecutive top-flight victory.

THE TEAMS

Burnley					Liverpool
	Pieters	McNeil		Alexander-Arnold	
	Mee c	Cork	Wood	Salah	Henderson c 71'	Matip
Pope			Firmino 85'	Fabinho	Adrián
	Tarkowski	Westwood	Barnes 73'	van Dijk	
	Lowton	Lennon	Mané 85'	Wijnaldum	Robertson

Used subs **Rodriguez** 73' ⬆   Used subs **Oxlade-Chamberlain** 71' ⬆ **Shaqiri** 85' ⬆ **Origi** 85' ⬆

"They were clinical today. Very good on transition which we know they are. We gave the ball away in so many dangerous positions and you can't do it against these because they will pounce. They wait for their moments and when they get their moments they hurt you. That was the biggest difference in the game, on transition."

Sean Dyche (Burnley manager)

"We were brilliant. There were so many 50-50 situations because of the long balls but we played early balls in behind as well… Everything was there. The intensity we put into games is unbelievable. I can ask for a lot but still the boys have to deliver, and they do… I told everyone that we want to create our own history and that is what the boys do week in, week out."

Jürgen Klopp

HOW THE LEAGUE WAS WON

Liverpool clinched their inaugural First Division Championship courtesy of victory in the final game of the season away to West Brom. Needing just a point to pip Sunderland, who had already completed their fixtures, a goal from Johnny Walker in the 20th minute was enough to secure victory and a first-ever title.

DROWNED 1900-1. WHO'S TURN NEXT?

Manager: Tom Watson
Captain: Alex Raisbeck
Top Scorer: Sam Raybould (17)
Most appearances: Bill Goldie, Bill Perkins, Tommy Robertson (34)
Number of players used: 18
Biggest victory: 5-0 v West Bromwich Albion (h)
Heaviest defeat: 0-3 v Notts County (a)
Average attendance: 15,647

		P	W	D	L	GF	GA	PTS
1	LIVERPOOL	34	19	7	8	59	35	45
2	SUNDERLAND	34	15	13	6	57	26	43
3	NOTTS COUNTY	34	18	4	12	54	46	40
4	NOTTINGHAM FOREST	34	16	7	11	53	36	39
5	BURY	34	16	7	11	53	37	39
6	NEWCASTLE UNITED	34	14	10	10	42	37	38
7	EVERTON	34	16	5	13	55	42	37
8	THE WEDNESDAY	34	13	10	11	52	42	36
9	BLACKBURN ROVERS	34	12	9	13	39	47	33
10	BOLTON WANDERERS	34	13	7	14	39	55	33
11	MANCHESTER CITY	34	13	6	15	48	58	32
12	DERBY COUNTY	34	12	7	15	55	42	31
13	WOLVERHAMPTON WANDERERS	34	9	13	12	39	55	31
14	SHEFFIELD UNITED	34	12	7	15	35	52	31
15	ASTON VILLA	34	10	10	14	45	51	30
16	STOKE CITY	34	11	5	18	46	57	27
17	PRESTON NORTH END	34	9	7	18	49	75	25
18	WEST BROMWICH ALBION	34	7	8	19	35	62	22

Alex Raisbeck, captain

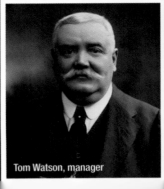

Tom Watson, manager

HOW THE LEAGUE WAS WON

With two games remaining Liverpool, league leaders since December, travelled to Bolton on Easter Monday knowing one more victory would clinch the title. Despite a 3-2 defeat at Burnden Park they returned home as champions due to the result at Roker Park where nearest challengers Preston lost 2-0 to Sunderland.

Liverpool Football Ground
The Wrench Series. No. 4468

Manager: **Tom Watson**
Captain: **Alex Raisbeck**
Top Scorer: **Joe Hewitt (24)**
Most appearances: **Arthur Goddard (38)**
Number of players used: **21**
Biggest victory: **6-1 v Middlesbrough (h)**
Heaviest defeat: **0-5 v Aston Villa (a)**
Average attendance: **17,736**

		P	W	D	L	GF	GA	PTS
1	LIVERPOOL	38	23	5	10	79	46	51
2	PRESTON NORTH END	38	17	13	8	54	39	47
3	THE WEDNESDAY	38	18	8	12	63	52	44
4	NEWCASTLE UNITED	38	18	7	13	74	48	43
5	MANCHESTER CITY	38	19	5	14	73	54	43
6	BOLTON WANDERERS	38	17	7	14	81	67	41
7	BIRMINGHAM	38	17	7	14	65	59	41
8	ASTON VILLA	38	17	6	15	72	56	40
9	BLACKBURN ROVERS	38	16	8	14	54	52	40
10	STOKE CITY	38	16	7	15	54	55	39
11	EVERTON	38	15	7	16	70	66	37
12	WOOLWICH ARSENAL	38	15	7	16	62	64	37
13	SHEFFIELD UNITED	38	15	6	17	57	62	36
14	SUNDERLAND	38	15	5	18	61	70	35
15	DERBY COUNTY	38	14	7	17	39	58	35
16	NOTTS COUNTY	38	11	12	15	55	71	34
17	BURY	38	11	10	17	57	74	32
18	MIDDLESBROUGH	38	10	11	17	56	71	31
19	NOTTINGHAM FOREST	38	13	5	20	58	79	31
20	WOLVERHAMPTON WANDERERS	38	8	7	23	58	99	23

Arthur Goddard

JOSEPH HEWITT (Liverpool F.C.)
Joe Hewitt

14

JORDAN
HENDERSON

Games	30
Goals	4
Assists	5

VIRGIL
VAN DIJK

4

Games	38
Goals	5
Assists	1

Saturday 14 September 2019 • Venue: Anfield • Attendance: 53,318 • Referee: Andre Marriner

LIVERPOOL 3 1 NEWCASTLE UTD

Mané (28, 40)
Salah (72)

Willems (7)

MATCH OVERVIEW

Liverpool recovered from the shock of conceding an early goal and went on to complete a routine win; their fifth in a row since the start of the season. A Mané brace saw them regain control by half-time time before Salah sealed the points in the second half.

THE TEAMS

Liverpool	Newcastle
Robertson	Krafth ⬇ 67'
	Almirón ⬇ 67'
Wijnaldum ⬇ 84'	Origi ⬇ 37'	Schär ⬇ 80'
van Dijk Ⓒ	Hayden
Adrián	Fabinho	Mané	Joelinton	Lascelles Ⓒ	Dubravka
Matip	Shelvey
Oxlade-Chamberlain ⬇ 75'	Salah	Dummett
	Atsu
Alexander-Arnold	Willems

Used subs **Firmino** 37' ⬆ **Milner** 75' ⬆ **Shaqiri** 84' ⬆

Used subs **Manquillo** 67' ⬆ **Mutu** 67' ⬆ **Fernandez** 80' ⬆

"I started enjoying it after 35 minutes when we arrived in the game. It was difficult. They had the speed to go in behind on the break, it was not easy. We had some time to set the rhythm, we had to play much quicker and then we had chances. We scored two wonderful goals. The challenge is always after the international break to find a common rhythm again."

Jürgen Klopp

"Liverpool are as good as you get. You can understand why they are European champions and lost once last year. They are an excellent, excellent team with pace and creativity and at the top end of the pitch they damage you. They are going to be there or thereabouts."

Steve Bruce (Newcastle manager)

Sunday 22 September 2019 • Venue: Stamford Bridge • Attendance: 40,638 • Referee: Michael Oliver

CHELSEA 1 2 LIVERPOOL

Kante (71)

Alexander-Arnold (14)
Firmino (30)

MATCH OVERVIEW

Liverpool came through their toughest test of the season yet with a victory that sent out an ominous warning to their title rivals. They got off to a flying start with two first-half goals, then successfully withstood a barrage of pressure to restore their five-point lead at the top.

THE TEAMS

Kepa

Emerson 15'
Tomori
Christensen 42'
Azpilicueta c

Kovacic
Jorginho
Kanté

Mount
Abraham 77'
Willian

Salah 90'
Firmino
Mané 72'

Henderson c
Fabinho
Wijnaldum

Alexander-Arnold
Matip
van Dijk
Robertson

Adrián

Used subs **Alonso** 15' **Zouma** 42' **Batshuayi** 77'

Used subs **Milner** 72' **Lallana** 84' **Gomez** 90'

"Obviously you can't expect to come to Stamford Bridge and have it all your own way. We were prepared to have it tough in the second half; they're at home, they're a proud side, they were always going to come out fighting. We started the second half quite well but the last 25 to 30 minutes were really tough. We had to defend well."

Trent Alexander-Arnold

"It was a really good performance and we scored two wonderful goals. It was an exciting game and it was intense. You will never win at Chelsea without putting a proper shift in, and I think we deserved the three points. The boys did really well, they fought really hard. I don't think there is any other way to win here. It's a big win."

Jürgen Klopp

SHEFFIELD UTD 0 1 LIVERPOOL

Wijnaldum (70)

MATCH OVERVIEW

Without being anywhere near their best, Liverpool returned home from Sheffield with their one hundred per cent record intact. A blunder by Blades' keeper Dean Henderson following a Gini Wijnaldum shot midway through the second half gifted them a fortuitous but vital victory.

THE TEAMS

Sheffield United

Henderson

O'Connell Egan Basham

Stevens Fleck Norwood c 77' Lundstram Baldock

McBurnie Robinson 60'

Liverpool

Adrián

Alexander-Arnold Matip van Dijk Robertson

Salah 90' Henderson c 84' Fabinho Wijnaldum

Firmino Mané 72'

Used subs **Mousset** 60' ⬆ **Clarke** 77' ⬆   Used subs **Origi** 63' ⬆ **Milner** 87' ⬆ **Oxlade-Chamberlain** 90' ⬆

"We had our moments and we started well but then lost the rhythm. All respect to Sheffield United, they did really well over 95 minutes. If it had been a draw, I would say that is what Sheffield deserved and we deserved."

Jürgen Klopp

"Liverpool had an off day and I think we missed an opportunity."

**Chris Wilder
(Sheffield United manager)**

"We're not at our best now but hopefully at the end of the season we will be. We slowed the game down too much and that's why they could stop our attacks... But another win, that's the most important thing."

Georginio Wijnaldum

Saturday 5 October 2019 • Venue: Anfield • Attendance: 53,322 • Referee: Chris Kavanagh

LIVERPOOL 2 1 LEICESTER CITY

Mané (40)   Maddison (80)
Milner (95)

MATCH OVERVIEW

A dramatic end to this game saw Leicester equalise ten minutes from time but just when it looked as though Liverpool would have to settle for a point, James Milner stepped up to coolly slot home an injury time penalty to keep the winning run going.

THE TEAMS

Liverpool

Adrián
Robertson
van Dijk c
Lovren
Alexander-Arnold
Milner
Fabinho
Wijnaldum 78'
Firmino 78'
Salah 90'
Mané

Used subs **Henderson** 78' ▲ **Origi** 78' ▲ **Lallana** 77' ▲

Leicester City

Schmeichel c
Pereira
Evans
Söyüncü
Chilwell
Praet 73'
Ndidi
Tielemans
Barnes 46'
Vardy
Maddison 86'

Used subs **Albrighton** 46' ▲ **Perez** 73' ▲ **Choudhury** 86' ▲

"Super game. The football we played for 60 minutes was incredible. And then we have the penalty situation. To score a penalty you need somebody who can keep his nerve and Millie is obviously the right guy for that after an impressive performance anyway. If winning eight games in a row would be easy, a whole lot of other teams would have done it… It is really difficult."

Jürgen Klopp

"We're just delighted to get the win; it was always going to be tough, they're a good team. We looked pretty tired in the second half but we found a way to win again. It shows the character of the squad. There was a bit of a wait. but I was just trying to stay calm and concentrate on what I was going to do."

James Milner

RETRO CHAMPS 1921/22

HOW THE LEAGUE WAS WON

Liverpool's third league title and their first in 16 years was confirmed following a 2-1 victory at home to Burnley. Dick Forshaw scored the winning goal that afternoon and with just three games left to play (in the days of two points for a win) it was a result that gave them an unassailable seven point lead over closest rivals Tottenham.

Manager: **Dave Ashworth**
Captain: **Ephraim Longworth**
Top Scorer: **Harry Chambers (19)**
Most appearances: **Dick Forshaw, Fred Hopkin (42)**
Number of players used: **22**
Biggest victory: **5-1 v Cardiff City (h)**
Heaviest defeat: **0-4 v Oldham Athletic (a)**
Average attendance: **37,142**

		P	W	D	L	GF	GA	PTS
1	LIVERPOOL	42	22	13	7	63	36	57
2	TOTTENHAM HOTSPUR	42	21	9	12	65	39	51
3	BURNLEY	42	22	5	15	72	54	49
4	CARDIFF CITY	42	19	10	13	61	53	48
5	ASTON VILLA	42	22	3	17	74	55	47
6	BOLTON WANDERERS	42	20	7	15	68	59	47
7	NEWCASTLE UNITED	42	18	10	14	59	45	46
8	MIDDLESBROUGH	42	16	14	12	79	69	46
9	CHELSEA	42	17	12	13	40	43	46
10	MANCHESTER CITY	42	18	9	15	65	70	45
11	SHEFFIELD UNITED	42	15	10	17	59	54	40
12	SUNDERLAND	42	16	8	18	60	62	40
13	WEST BROMWICH ALBION	42	15	10	17	51	63	40
14	HUDDERSFIELD TOWN	42	15	9	18	53	54	39
15	BLACKBURN ROVERS	42	13	12	17	54	57	38
16	PRESTON NORTH END	42	13	12	17	42	65	38
17	ARSENAL	42	15	7	20	47	56	37
18	BIRMINGHAM	42	15	7	20	48	60	37
19	OLDHAM ATHLETIC	42	13	11	18	38	50	37
20	EVERTON	42	12	12	18	57	55	36
21	BRADFORD CITY	42	11	10	21	48	72	32
22	MANCHESTER UNITED	42	8	12	22	41	73	28

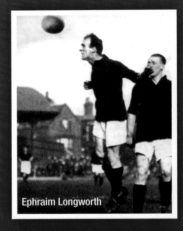

Ephraim Longworth

Harry Chambers

RETRO CHAMPS 1922/23

HOW THE LEAGUE WAS WON

A 1-1 home draw with Huddersfield was enough to see Liverpool confirmed as back-to-back champions for the first time in the club's history. Harry Chambers struck the equalising goal that secured the all-important point which, coupled with a defeat for second-placed Sunderland on the same afternoon, ensured that even with two games still to play, the Reds' lead at the top was insurmountable.

Anfield

Manager: **Dave Ashworth/Matt McQueen**
Captain: **Donald Mackinlay**
Top Scorer: **Harry Chambers (22)**
Most appearances: **Dick Forshaw, Elisha Scott, Donald Mackinlay**
Number of players used: **19**
Biggest victory: **5-1 v Sunderland (h)**
Heaviest defeat: **1-4 v Sheffield United (a)**
Average attendance: **33,872**

		P	W	D	L	GF	GA	PTS
1	**LIVERPOOL**	42	26	8	8	70	31	60
2	**SUNDERLAND**	42	22	10	10	72	54	54
3	**HUDDERSFIELD TOWN**	42	21	11	10	60	32	53
4	**NEWCASTLE UNITED**	42	18	12	12	45	37	48
5	**EVERTON**	42	20	7	15	63	59	47
6	**ASTON VILLA**	42	18	10	14	64	51	46
7	**WEST BROMWICH ALBION**	42	17	11	14	58	49	45
8	**MANCHESTER CITY**	42	17	11	14	50	49	45
9	**CARDIFF CITY**	42	18	7	17	73	59	43
10	**SHEFFIELD UNITED**	42	16	10	16	68	64	42
11	**ARSENAL**	42	16	10	16	61	62	42
12	**TOTTENHAM HOTSPUR**	42	17	7	18	50	50	41
13	**BOLTON WANDERERS**	42	14	12	16	50	58	40
14	**BLACKBURN ROVERS**	42	14	12	16	47	62	40
15	**BURNLEY**	42	16	6	20	58	59	38
16	**PRESTON NORTH END**	42	13	11	18	60	64	37
17	**BIRMINGHAM**	42	13	11	18	41	57	37
18	**MIDDLESBROUGH**	42	13	10	19	57	63	36
19	**CHELSEA**	42	9	18	15	45	53	36
20	**NOTTINGHAM FOREST**	42	13	8	21	41	70	34
21	**STOKE CITY**	42	10	10	22	47	67	30
22	**OLDHAM ATHLETIC**	42	10	10	22	35	65	30

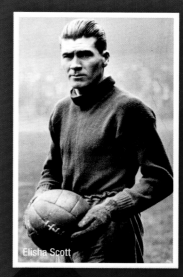
Elisha Scott

Don Mackinlay

9

ROBERTO
FIRMINO

Games	38
Goals	9
Assists	8

66

TRENT
ALEXANDER-ARNOLD

Games	38
Goals	4
Assists	13

MATCHDAY NINE

Sunday 20 October 2019 • Venue: Old Trafford • Attendance: 73,737 • Referee: Martin Atkinson

MAN UTD 1 1 LIVERPOOL

Rashford (36) Lallana (85)

MATCH OVERVIEW

Adam Lallana came off the bench to rescue a point for Liverpool in a game marred by controversial VAR decisions. Lallana netted to cancel out Rashford's first-half opener and although the result ended Liverpool's winning start to the season this was certainly a point gained rather than two lost.

THE TEAMS

Young c

Rojo

Fred   Rashford
                        84'
de Gea   Maguire   Pereira
                        90'
          McTominay   James
Lindelöf
          Wan-Bissaka

Alexander-Arnold

Mané   Henderson c
          71'   Matip
Firmino   Fabinho
                                 Alisson
                      van Dijk
Origi   Wijnaldum
59'   82'
          Robertson

Used subs Martial 84' Williams 90'   **Used subs** Oxlade-Chamberlain 59' Lallana 71' Keïta 82'

"They were better than us and defended well, but in the end they scored a goal that shows all the problems with VAR. We then scored a goal that was disallowed. Pretty much everything went against us today, but we still didn't lose. We deserved the point, 100 per cent."

"We probably weren't at our best today but sometimes you have to look to the bench and you have to come on and change the game. If we're going to compete to take the title then we're not just going to need 11, we're going to need a squad. Towards the end, I thought we were the only team that was going to get three points."

Jürgen Klopp **Adam Lallana**

Sunday 27 October 2019 • Venue: Anfield • Attendance: 53,222 • Referee: Anthony Taylor

LIVERPOOL **2** **1** TOTTENHAM

Henderson (52)
Salah (75)

Kane (1)

MATCH OVERVIEW

In what was the first meeting between these teams since the previous season's Champions League final, Liverpool's fighting qualities were evident once again as they bounced back from the blow of conceding an early goal to eventually run out deserved winners in a hard-fought encounter.

THE TEAMS

Liverpool

Alisson

Robertson
van Dijk
Lovren
Alexander-Arnold

Wijnaldum 77'
Fabinho
Henderson c

Mané
Firmino 90'
Salah 85'

Used subs **Milner** 77' **Gomez** 85' **Origi** 90'

Tottenham

Gazzaniga

Aurier 84'
Alderweireld
Sanchez
Rose

Eriksen 88'
Kane c
Son

Sissoko
Winks 63'
Alli

Used subs **Ndombele** 63' **Moura** 84' **Celso** 88'

"That was us at our best. That's how football should look, how we should play against a strong, organised side, with the threat that every ball you lose could end up in front of your own goal. The counter-press was exceptional. I loved that, it was really, really good. We won it, and we deserved it, and I'm really happy about the performance."

Jürgen Klopp

"Our mentality has improved. That's grown over the last few years and the gaffer has changed that so much. We have faced adversity at times. It's not always going to go your own way. After 48 seconds I was thinking it was my fault because I gave the ball away for their goal. Thankfully I managed to get a goal to make up for it."

Jordan Henderson

Saturday 2 November 2019 • Venue: Villa Park • Attendance: 41,878 • Referee: Jonathon Moss

ASTON VILLA 1 2 LIVERPOOL

Trezequet (21)

Robertson (87)
Mané (90)

MATCH OVERVIEW

On what was a significant day in the title race, Liverpool were staring a first defeat in the face until a stunning comeback, instigated by Andy Robertson's 87th minute equaliser and completed by Sadio Mané's injury time winner, dramatically turned things around to preserve the six-point advantage at the top.

THE TEAMS

AVFC

Targett

Mings c

Luiz ⬇ 73'

Trézéguet

Salah ⬇ 65'

Henderson c

Alexander-Arnold

Mings c

Nakamba

Wesley ⬇ 86'

Firmino

Lallana ⬇ 84'

Lovren

Heaton

Engels

Mané

Alisson

Guilbert ⬇ 69'

McGinn

El Ghazi

Mané

Wijnaldum ⬇ 65'

van Dijk

Robertson

Used subs El Mohamady 69' • Hourihane 73' • Kodjia 86' ⬆

Used subs Oxlade-Chamberlain 65' ⬆ Origi 65' ⬆ Keïta 84' ⬆

"We had our good moments during the game but were not clinical enough. After the first half we realised we were on the wrong path and we made changes… on days like this you just need to be ready to fight."

Jürgen Klopp

"We have showed our resilience over the last 18 months and this season we have kept on going. Today we knew we had some great chances and there's nothing better than a last-minute winner."

Andy Robertson

"Today was not our best performance but we deserved the three points. It was a perfect delivery from the corner and in the end I was even a bit lucky the ball went in."

Sadio Mané

MATCHDAY TWELVE

Sunday 10 November 2019 • Venue: Anfield • Attendance: 53,324 • Referee: Michael Oliver

LIVERPOOL 3 1 MAN CITY

Fabinho (6)   Mané (51)   Bernardo (78)
Salah (13)

MATCH OVERVIEW

In a pulsating encounter that lived up to the pre-match hype, Liverpool romped to victory against the reigning champions and, in opening up a nine-point lead over City, issued the strongest statement of intent yet that this could finally be their year.

THE TEAMS

LIVERPOOL

Robertson
Wijnaldum   Mané
van Dijk
Alisson   Fabinho   Firmino 79'
Lovren
Henderson c 61'   Salah 87'
Alexander-Arnold

MAN CITY

Walker
B.Silva
Rodrigo
Stones
Agüero 71'   De Bruyne
Bravo
Fernandinho c
Gündogan
Sterling
Angeliño

Used subs **Milner** 61' ⬆ **Oxlade-Chamberlain** 79' ⬆ **Gomez** 87' ⬆   Used subs **Jesus** 71' ⬆

"We were today completely focused on this game and not the situation in the table or how many points we are ahead of City. That's crazy. Nine points, you cannot imagine that something like this happens, but it is not important. We want to be first in May and not only in November. We just try what we can and in the end we will see what happens."

Jürgen Klopp

"Congratulations to Liverpool, they scored three, we got one but I'm proud of my team; few teams can come here and play the way that we did against the strongest team in Europe. We cannot deny how good Liverpool are but the way we played, the personality, it was good. It was an honour for both teams to show the Premier League spectators this type of game."

Pep Guardiola (Manchester City manager)

HOW THE LEAGUE WAS WON

After completing their league season with a crucial 2-1 victory away to fellow title challengers Wolves on 31 May, Liverpool had to endure an agonising two-week wait before Stoke City's defeat at Sheffield United confirmed the Reds – rank outsiders at the start of the season – as the inaugural post-war champions.

Manager: George Kay
Captain: Willie Fagan
Top Scorer: Albert Stubbins & Jack Balmer (24)
Most appearances: Jack Balmer (39)
Number of players used: 26
Biggest victory: 6-1 v Grimsby Town (a)
Heaviest defeat: 0-5 v Manchester United (a)
Average attendance: 45,731

		P	W	D	L	GF	GA	PTS
1	LIVERPOOL	42	25	7	10	84	52	57
2	MANCHESTER UNITED	42	22	12	8	95	54	56
3	WOLVERHAMPTON WANDERERS	42	25	6	11	98	56	56
4	STOKE CITY	42	24	7	11	90	53	55
5	BLACKPOOL	42	22	6	14	71	70	50
6	SHEFFIELD UNITED	42	21	7	14	89	75	49
7	PRESTON NORTH END	42	18	11	13	76	74	47
8	ASTON VILLA	42	18	9	15	67	53	45
9	SUNDERLAND	42	18	8	16	65	66	44
10	EVERTON	42	17	9	16	62	67	43
11	MIDDLESBROUGH	42	17	8	17	73	68	42
12	PORTSMOUTH	42	16	9	17	66	60	41
13	ARSENAL	42	16	9	17	72	70	41
14	DERBY COUNTY	42	18	5	19	73	79	41
15	CHELSEA	42	16	7	19	69	84	39
16	GRIMSBY TOWN	42	13	12	17	61	82	38
17	BLACKBURN ROVERS	42	14	8	20	45	53	36
18	BOLTON WANDERERS	42	13	8	21	57	69	34
19	CHARLTON ATHLETIC	42	11	12	19	57	71	34
20	HUDDERSFIELD TOWN	42	13	7	22	53	79	33
21	BRENTFORD	42	9	7	26	45	88	25
22	LEEDS UNITED	42	6	6	30	45	90	18

George Kay

Willie Fagan

RETRO CHAMPS 1963/64

HOW THE LEAGUE WAS WON

The first League Championship of Bill Shankly's managerial reign was wrapped up in style with four games to spare on a glorious sunny afternoon at Anfield. Arsenal were the opponents and they offered no resistance against a rampant Liverpool side who rose to the occasion by scoring five goals without reply.

Manager: Bill Shankly
Captain: Ron Yeats
Top Scorer: **Roger Hunt (31)**
Most appearances: **Ian Callaghan, Gordon Milne, Peter Thompson (42)**
Number of players used: **17**
Biggest victory: **6-0 v Wolverhampton Wanders (h) & Ipswich Town (h)**
Heaviest defeat: **0-3 v Sheffield United (a)**
Average attendance: **45,031**

		P	W	D	L	GF	GA	PTS
1	LIVERPOOL	42	26	5	11	92	45	57
2	MANCHESTER UNITED	42	23	7	12	90	62	53
3	EVERTON	42	21	10	11	84	64	52
4	TOTTENHAM HOTSPUR	42	22	7	13	97	81	51
5	CHELSEA	42	20	10	12	72	56	50
6	SHEFFIELD WEDNESDAY	42	19	11	12	84	67	49
7	BLACKBURN ROVERS	42	18	10	14	89	65	46
8	ARSENAL	42	17	11	14	90	82	45
9	BURNLEY	42	17	10	15	71	64	44
10	WEST BROMWICH ALBION	42	16	11	15	70	61	43
11	LEICESTER CITY	42	16	11	15	61	58	43
12	SHEFFIELD UNITED	42	16	11	15	61	64	43
13	NOTTINGHAM FOREST	42	16	9	17	64	68	41
14	WEST HAM UNITED	42	14	12	16	69	74	40
15	FULHAM	42	13	13	16	58	65	39
16	WOLVERHAMPTON WANDERERS	42	12	15	15	70	80	39
17	STOKE CITY	42	14	10	18	77	78	38
18	BLACKPOOL	42	13	9	20	52	73	35
19	ASTON VILLA	42	11	12	19	62	71	34
20	BIRMINGHAM CITY	42	11	7	24	54	92	29
21	BOLTON WANDERERS	42	10	8	24	48	80	28
22	IPSWICH TOWN	42	9	7	26	56	121	25

Bill Shankly

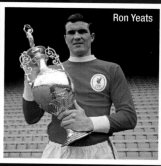

Ron Yeats

5

GEORGINIO
WIJNALDUM

Games	37
Goals	4
Assists	0

26

ANDY
ROBERTSON

Games	36
Goals	2
Assists	12

CRYSTAL PALACE 1   2 LIVERPOOL

Zaha (82)

Mané (49)
Firmino (85)

MATCH OVERVIEW

Liverpool's unbeaten Premier League march continued with more late drama. This time it was Bobby Firmino who emerged the hero, firing home the winning goal just three minutes after Palace had drawn level. It extended Liverpool's run of games without defeat in the league to 30 and kept them eight points clear at the top.

THE TEAMS

Crystal Palace

van Aanholt   McArthur
Cahill   Zaha
Guaita   Milivojevic c
Tomkins   Ayew 76'
Townsend
Ward 70'   Kouyaté 72'

Used subs **Kelly** 70' ⬆ **Schlupp** 72' ⬆ **Benteke** 76' ⬆

Liverpool

Alexander-Arnold
Henderson c 79'
Mané   Lovren
Firmino 89'   Fabinho   Alisson
Oxlade-Chamberlain 64'   van Dijk
Wijnaldum   Robertson

Used subs **Origi** 64' ⬆ **Milner** 79' ⬆ **Gomez** 89' ⬆

"Today, I have no problem that we were not brilliant because in a game like this you just have to make sure you're ready to fight for the result and we were that from the first minute. Could we have played better? Yes, but getting a result at Crystal Palace, you never take for granted. So, it feels good."

Jürgen Klopp

"The first game back after an international is always difficult because you go away and you play a different style. You've got players travelling all over the world and obviously a bit of jetlag in there. We've performed not at our best but we've got the win. That's what good teams do, find a way to win, and that's what we have done."

Trent Alexander-Arnold

LIVERPOOL 2 1 BRIGHTON & HOVE ALBION

van Dijk (18, 24)

Dunk (79)

MATCH OVERVIEW

Not even the 78th minute dismissal of goalkeeper Alisson could derail the Liverpool title-chasing bandwagon, as another three points were successfully banked. The Reds were cruising after van Dijk's first-half double but nerves became frayed when the visitors pulled a late goal back and there was widespread relief when the final whistle sounded.

THE TEAMS

Liverpool:
Alisson
van Dijk
Lovren
Robertson
Alexander-Arnold
Wijnaldum
Henderson c
Oxlade-Chamberlain 78'
Mané
Firmino 76'
Salah 69'

Brighton:
Ryan
Webster
Dunk c
Burn
Montoya 69'
Pröpper
Stephens
Mooy
Groß
Connolly 76'
Bissouma 69'

Used subs **Lallana** 69' **Origi** 76' **Adrián** 78'

Used subs **Alzate** 69' **Trossard** 69' **Maupay** 76'

"I'm very, very happy with the effort the boys put in again. I'm really happy and proud of the desire they showed. The red card made it a really special win, to be honest. Results-wise, it's an incredible period, for sure. But we don't want to think about the last 14 games. We are only concerned about the next one."

Jürgen Klopp

"They are a very good side, you have to give them credit. They played well, brave, and tried to get out of our press and at times it worked. But we wanted the three points and got them. We have to show character, we have to fight. It was not an easy game, especially at the end. We had to dig deep and we did."

Virgil van Dijk

Wednesday 4 December 2019 • Venue: Anfield • Attendance: 53,094 • Referee: Mike Dean

LIVERPOOL 5 2 EVERTON

Origi (6, 31)   Mané (45)
Shaqiri (19)   Wijnaldum (90)

Keane (21)
Richarlison (45)

MATCH OVERVIEW

Liverpool's reign as the pride of Merseyside remained firmly in place after this latest demolition of the Blues. At one point it looked like being a cricket score as they netted four times before the break and although the goals then dried up, Gini Wijnaldum capped a memorable night by adding a fifth in the final minute.

THE TEAMS

Liverpool

Adrián
van Dijk
Lovren
Robertson
Alexander-Arnold 83'
Milner (c)
Wijnaldum
Mané
Lallana 72'
Shaqiri
Origi 73'

Everton

Pickford
Holgate
Keane
Mina
Digne
Sidibé 35'
Davies 72'
Sigurdsson (c)
Iwobi
Calvert-Lewin 60'
Richarlison

Used subs **Henderson** 72' **Firmino** 73' **Gomez** 83'

Used subs **Bernard** 35' **Kean** 60' **Schneiderlin** 72'

"All the goals were incredible, outstanding. Wonderful goals, sensational passes, super pieces of football. I loved it a lot! We needed fresh legs and I had to show my respect to the boys in the squad, that's all. They proved it."

Jürgen Klopp

"It was a really good day for us. We did very well. It's big credit for the team; you can see how good we are."

Xherdan Shaqiri

"Bad game for us, really bad night for us as well. They deserved the three points, there's no doubt about that. Every time they went forward they almost had a chance to score and it was really tough for us."

**Marco Silva
(Everton manager)**

Saturday 7 December 2019 • Venue: Dean Court • Attendance: 10,832 • Referee: Chris Kavanagh

BOURNEMOUTH 0 3 LIVERPOOL

Oxlade-Chamberlain (35)
Keïta (44)
Salah (54)

MATCH OVERVIEW

Liverpool strolled to victory on the south coast to further strengthen their position at the Premier League summit. The game was all but over by half-time thanks to goals from Alex Oxlade-Chamberlain and Naby Keïta, and within ten minutes of the restart Mo Salah added a third to make sure.

THE TEAMS

Bournemouth	Liverpool
Ramsdale	Alisson
Rico	Gomez
Fraser	Keïta
Ake 35'	Salah
Biling 58'	Lovren 40'
Wilson 64'	Henderson c
Mepham	van Dijk
Lerma	Firmino
Solanke	Milner
Francis c	Oxlade-Chamberlain 87'
Groeneveld	Robertson 76'

Used subs Simpson 35' • Cook 58' • Gosling 64'

Used subs Alexander-Arnold 40' • Jones 76' • Shaqiri 87'

"The boys made a lot of good decisions and that's why it was a comfortable win, maybe more than we would have expected before the game. We scored wonderful goals and had other big chances. The result is most important, but the performance was really good as well. There were not a lot of difficult moments to defend, which is very important, so nearly a perfect day."

Jürgen Klopp

"It was really professional from start to finish and I think it was probably the main thing we needed to improve on. In weeks gone by, we have gone 2-0 up and we just haven't controlled the game well enough and we've made it difficult. Today, we learned from that and it was a just a really good performance from everyone."

Alex Oxlade-Chamberlain

RETRO CHAMPS 1965/66

HOW THE LEAGUE WAS WON

Long-time league leaders Liverpool went into their final home game requiring just one more point to clinch a second title in three years. Such was the inevitability of the outcome, opponents Chelsea welcomed them onto the pitch with a guard of honour, before Roger Hunt scored twice in a 2-1 win.

Manager: **Bill Shankly**
Captain: **Ron Yeats**
Top Scorer: **Roger Hunt (29)**
Most appearances: **Gerry Byrne, Ian Callaghan, Tommy Lawrence, Tommy Smith, Ron Yeats (42)**
Number of players used: **14**
Biggest victory: **5-0 v Everton (h) & Northampton Town (h)**
Heaviest defeat: **0-3 v West Bromwich Albion (a)**
Average attendance: **46,334**

		P	W	D	L	GF	GA	PTS
1	LIVERPOOL	42	26	9	7	79	34	61
2	LEEDS UNITED	42	23	9	10	79	38	55
3	BURNLEY	42	24	7	11	79	47	55
4	MANCHESTER UNITED	42	18	15	9	84	59	51
5	CHELSEA	42	22	7	13	65	53	51
6	WEST BROMWICH ALBION	42	19	12	11	91	69	50
7	LEICESTER CITY	42	21	7	14	80	65	49
8	TOTTENHAM HOTSPUR	42	16	12	14	75	66	44
9	SHEFFIELD UNITED	42	16	11	15	56	59	43
10	STOKE CITY	42	15	12	15	65	64	42
11	EVERTON	42	15	11	16	56	62	41
12	WEST HAM UNITED	42	15	9	18	70	83	39
13	BLACKPOOL	42	14	9	19	55	65	37
14	ARSENAL	42	12	13	17	62	75	37
15	NEWCASTLE UNITED	42	14	9	19	50	63	37
16	ASTON VILLA	42	15	6	21	69	80	36
17	SHEFFIELD WEDNESDAY	42	14	8	20	56	66	36
18	NOTTINGHAM FOREST	42	14	8	20	56	72	36
19	SUNDERLAND	42	14	8	20	51	72	36
20	FULHAM	42	14	7	21	67	85	35
21	NORTHAMPTON TOWN	42	10	13	19	55	92	33
22	BLACKBURN ROVERS	42	8	4	30	57	88	20

Roger Hunt

HOW THE LEAGUE WAS WON

Shankly's second great Liverpool team came of age on the last Saturday of the league season when a goalless draw at home to Leicester gave them the point needed to confirm the club's eighth First Division Championship – a tally that only Arsenal could match.

Manager: Bill Shankly
Captain: Tommy Smith
Top Scorer: Kevin Keegan & John Toshack (13)
Most appearances: Ian Callaghan, Chris Lawler, Larry Lloyd (42)
Number of players used: 16
Biggest victory: 5-0 v Sheffield United (h)
Heaviest defeat: 0-2 v Manchester United (a) & Arsenal (h)
Average attendance: 48,103

		P	W	D	L	GF	GA	PTS
1	LIVERPOOL	42	25	10	7	72	42	60
2	ARSENAL	42	23	11	8	57	43	57
3	LEEDS UNITED	42	21	11	10	71	45	53
4	IPSWICH TOWN	42	17	14	11	55	45	48
5	WOLVERHAMPTON WANDERERS	42	18	11	13	66	54	47
6	WEST HAM UNITED	42	17	12	13	67	53	46
7	DERBY COUNTY	42	19	8	15	56	54	46
8	TOTTENHAM HOTSPUR	42	16	13	13	58	48	45
9	NEWCASTLE UNITED	42	16	13	13	60	51	45
10	BIRMINGHAM CITY	42	15	12	15	53	54	42
11	MANCHESTER CITY	42	15	11	16	57	60	41
12	CHELSEA	42	13	14	15	49	51	40
13	SOUTHAMPTON	42	11	18	13	47	52	40
14	SHEFFIELD UNITED	42	15	10	17	51	59	40
15	STOKE CITY	42	14	10	18	61	56	38
16	LEICESTER CITY	42	10	17	15	40	46	37
17	EVERTON	42	13	11	18	41	49	37
18	MANCHESTER UNITED	42	12	13	17	44	60	37
19	COVENTRY CITY	42	13	9	20	40	55	35
20	NORWICH CITY	42	11	10	21	36	63	32
21	CRYSTAL PALACE	42	9	12	21	41	58	30
22	WEST BROMWICH ALBION	42	9	10	23	38	62	28

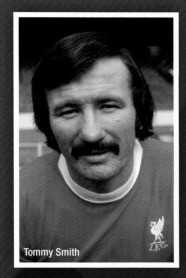

Tommy Smith

10

SADIO
MANÉ

Games	35
Goals	18
Assists	7

MO
SALAH

Games	34
Goals	19
Assists	10

DID YOU KNOW?

11 CHAMPION FACTS

1. Liverpool have now been crowned champions of England in eight different decades (the 1900s, 1920s, 1940s, 1960s, 1970s, 1980s, 1990s and the 2020s) – more than any other club.

2. The 30 year wait between the league title triumphs of 1990 and 2020 is the longest Liverpool have ever gone without being champions. The previous top three longest spells without a title were...

   - **24 years** – 1923 to 1947
   - **17 years** – 1947 to 1964
   - **16 years** – 1906 to 1922

3. Only five other clubs have endured a longer wait between titles than Liverpool. They are....

   - Blackburn Rovers 1914 to 1995 – **81 years**
   - Aston Villa 1910 to 1981 – **71 years**
   - Chelsea 1955 to 2005 – **50 years**
   - Manchester City 1968 to 2012 – **44 years**
   - Burnley 1921 to 1960 – **39 years**

4. Between October 2019 and February 2020, the Reds won 18 consecutive league matches, a joint-record by any club in the English top flight. This run came after Klopp's men had also embarked upon a 17-match winning streak between March and October 2019, which is also the third-longest such run in the Premier League.

Date of last game	Team	Run
24/02/2020	**Liverpool**	18
27/12/2017	**Manchester City**	18
05/10/2019	**Liverpool**	17
10/09/2019	**Manchester City**	15
18/08/2002	**Arsenal**	14
31/12/2016	**Chelsea**	13
05/03/1892	**Preston North End**	13
02/04/1892	**Sunderland**	13
01/10/1960	**Tottenham Hotspur**	13

5. Virgil van Dijk is only the fifth outfield player in Premier League history to play every minute of a title-winning campaign.

6. Liverpool achieved an unbeaten run of 44 Premier League matches from January 2019 to February 2020 – second only in the history of England's top division to Arsenal's 49-game run that ended in 2004.

7. From 9 February 2019 to 5 July 2020, the Reds won all 24 of their home games in the Premier League, surpassing their own previous top-flight record of 21 home wins in a row set under Bill Shankly in 1972. The run came to an end following the 1-1 draw with Burnley on 11 July 2020

8. In 2019-20, Liverpool defeated all 19 of the other teams in the Premier League, the last being West Ham in January. By that stage, the Reds had won 23 of their first 24 Premier League games of the campaign and had beaten every other side they had faced in a single top-flight season for the very first time in the club's history.

9. Jürgen Klopp is the ninth different manager to lead Liverpool to a league title – following in the footsteps of Tom Watson, Dave Ashworth, Matt McQueen, George Kay, Bill Shankly, Bob Paisley, Joe Fagan and Kenny Dalglish.

Leaderboard of Liverpool's title-winning managers

- Paisley – 6
- Shankly/Dalglish – 3
- Watson – 2
- Ashworth/McQueen/Kay/Fagan/Klopp – 1

10. Jordan Henderson also joins an elite band of Liverpool players to have lifted the league title as captain – something only Alex Raisbeck, Ephraim Longworth, Don Mackinlay, Willie Fagan, Ron Yeats, Tommy Smith, Emlyn Hughes, Phil Thompson, Graeme Souness and Alan Hansen have previously experienced.

Leaderboard of Liverpool's title-winning captains

- Souness/Hansen – 3
- Raisbeck/Yeats/Hughes/Thompson – 2
- Longworth/Mackinlay/Fagan/Smith – 1

11. Liverpool were confirmed as Premier League champions with seven games of their season left to play – this is the most fixtures remaining of any side upon confirming the English top-flight title in history.

Earliest Top-Flight Title Wins (Games)

Season	Champions	Games Remaining
2019/20	Liverpool	7
1907/08	Manchester United	5
1984/85	Everton	5
2000/01	Manchester United	5
2017/81	Manchester City	4
1908/09	Newcastle United	4
1919/20	West Bromwich Albion	4
1929/30	Sheffield Wednesday	4
1947/48	Arsenal	4
1978/79	Nottingham Forest	4
1987/88	Liverpool	4
1999/00	Manchester United	4
2003/04	Arsenal	4
2012/13	Manchester United	4

Saturday 14 December 2019 • Venue: Anfield • Attendance: 53,311 • Referee: Andre Marriner

LIVERPOOL 2 0 WATFORD

Salah (38, 90)

MATCH OVERVIEW

Two moments of magic from Mo Salah sealed a hard-earned win, but equally important was a first clean sheet of the season at home. Watford's performance belied their lowly league position but although the points were hanging in the balance until the final minute Liverpool ultimately had too much quality.

THE TEAMS

Liverpool

Alisson

van Dijk
Gomez
Milner
Alexander-Arnold

Wijnaldum 59'
Henderson c
Shaqiri 70'

Mané
Firmino 88'
Salah

Watford

Foster

Mariappa
Kabasele
Cathcart
Femenia

Capoue
Hughes

Sarr
Deeney c 75'
Doucouré 87'
Deulofeu

Used subs **Robertson** 59' ▲ **Oxlaide-Chamberlain** 70' ◆ **Origi** 88' ▲

Used subs **Gray** 75' ▲ **Quina** 87' ▲

"I think I've said it 500 times: December, January especially, you need to show a resilience, that's the most important thing. We showed that, but so did Watford. We had to fight, that's what we did and that's why we won. All good. You can make early judgements, but we can't. We just have to recover and go onto the next game."

Jürgen Klopp

"Sometimes you've just got to scrap it out, it can't always be nice and pretty football. But that's an important result today to get those three points in the way we did, battling it out. This team is so good at that, really good mentality. We want to win every game and keep pushing. You can see the quality in the squad because changes are being made all the time."

James Milner

Thursday 26 December 2019 • Venue: Leicester City Stadium • Attendance: 32,211 • Referee: Michael Oliver

LEICESTER CITY 0 4 LIVERPOOL

Firmino (31, 74)   Alexander-Arnold (78)
Milner (71)

MATCH OVERVIEW

The newly crowned club world champions marked their return to Premier League action in scintillating style on a Boxing Night that will long be remembered. Against their nearest challengers in the league, Liverpool totally outclassed the second-placed Foxes to move 13 points clear at the top of the table.

THE TEAMS

Leicester City

Schmeichel (c)

Chilwell
Söyüncü
Evans
Pereira

Maddison 76'
Tielemans
Ndidi
Praet 72'
Barnes 58'

Vardy

Used subs **Albrighton** 58' ▲ **Perez** 72' ▲ **Choudhury** 76' ▲

Liverpool

Salah 70'
Firmino
Mané

Keïta 70'
Henderson (c) 82'
Wijnaldum

Alexander-Arnold
Gomez
van Dijk
Robertson

Alisson

Used subs **Milner** 70' ▲ **Origi** 70' ▲ **Lallana** 82' ▲

"They are going to be very, very hard to stop, there's no doubt. Fantastic team. Confidence is high as well. They have become winners now and haven't lost many games over an 18-month period. They have got enough players now, enough experience and enough quality, to stay focused and get the job done."

Brendan Rodgers (Leicester manager)

"It was exactly the performance we needed. I think a little bit less good and we would have had problems. We had no real problems in the game because the boys were really 100 per cent in the game and that helped us a lot. We play Wolves, Sheffield United, Everton, Tottenham and Manchester United in our next five games. It doesn't sound like anything is decided in my ears."

Jürgen Klopp

LIVERPOOL 1 0 WOLVERHAMPTON WANDERERS

Mané (42)

MATCH OVERVIEW

Liverpool ended 2019 with a hard-earned win against one of the form teams in the league. Controversy surrounding VAR once again dominated the headlines, but the Reds headed into 2020 with an almost faultless record in the Premier League and their 13-point advantage intact.

THE TEAMS

Liverpool

Alisson

van Dijk
Gomez

Robertson
Wijnaldum 59'
Henderson c
Alexander-Arnold

Mané
Firmino 88'   Salah
Lallana 70'

Wolverhampton Wanderers

Neto
Jota 72'

Jonny
Dendoncker 58'
Neves 58'
Moutinho
Vinagre

Bennett
Coady c   Patricio
Kilman

Used subs **Keïta** 67' ⬆ **Milner** 86' ⬆ **Origi** 86' ⬆

Used subs **Saiss** 58' ⬆ **Traore** 58' ⬆ **Jimenez** 72' ⬆

"My 2019 was brilliant but it's not important because we count seasons not years, so the 2019-20 season is not over. We are halfway there, we still have 19 games to play and probably 18 or 19 of them will be like this tonight, for different reasons. We just created a basis which we will work with from now on, that's all."

Jürgen Klopp

"It's never easy for both sides to play in the circumstances – last week and this week a lot of games, travelling for both sides. They made it tough for us and we're obviously very happy that we kept the three points. You have to be very patient, you have to stay positive. We're in the middle of the season, halfway through, so we want to achieve more and more."

Virgil van Dijk

Thursday 2 January 2020 • Venue: Anfield • Attendance: 53,321 • Referee: Paul Tierney

LIVERPOOL 2 0 SHEFFIELD UTD

Salah (4)
Mané (64)

MATCH OVERVIEW

The new year began like the old one ended, with Liverpool taking another important step forward in their quest to become champions. Goals by Mo Salah and Sadio Mané brought the festive fixtures to a successful conclusion as the Reds completed a full calendar year unbeaten in the Premier League.

THE TEAMS

LIVERPOOL

Alisson

Robertson 88'
van Dijk
Gomez
Alexander-Arnold

Wijnaldum
Henderson c
Milner

Mané 78'
Firmino
Salah 90'

SHEFFIELD UNITED F.C. 1889

Baldock
Lundstram
Norwood c 78'
Fleck
Stevens

Basham
McGoldrick 66'
Mousset 65'
Egan
Henderson
O'Connell

Used subs **Origi** 78' **Lallana** 88' **Elliott** 90'

Used subs **McBurnie** 65' **Sharp** 66' **Besic** 78'

"We played in the exact way you have to play against Sheffield United. That was the best thing the boys did, they didn't let them get anything out of the game, which is really difficult. It's an intense period of the year but in terms of an overall performance it was as good as anything, really, really good. That makes me happy."

Jürgen Klopp

"You just look at the appetite and the desire of everybody around the football club; it's got a feeling of relentlessness about them and the supporters as well, the way they drive their players on. They realise what a huge, important season it is and a fantastic position they're in. It'd be a very brave man to bet against them being the champions of this division."

Chris Wilder (Sheffield United manager)

HOW THE LEAGUE WAS WON

Bob Paisley's first title as manager came on an unforgettable night at Molineux. In the final fixture of the season, Liverpool required a win to become champions, while Wolves needed the points to stay up. It was billed as the 'Great First Division Drama' and goals from Keegan, Toshack and Kennedy clinched a famous 3-1 victory.

Manager: **Bob Paisley**
Captain: **Emlyn Hughes**
Top Scorer: **John Toshack (16)**
Most appearances: **Ray Clemence, Phil Neal (42)**
Number of players used: **19**
Biggest victory: **4-0 v Tottenham Hotspur (a) & West Ham United (a)**
Heaviest defeat: **0-2 v Queens Park Rangers (a), Ipswich Town (a) & Middlesbrough (h)**
Average attendance: **41,670**

		P	W	D	L	GF	GA	PTS
1	**LIVERPOOL**	42	23	14	5	66	31	60
2	QUEENS PARK RANGERS	42	24	11	7	67	33	59
3	MANCHESTER UNITED	42	23	10	9	68	42	56
4	DERBY COUNTY	42	21	11	10	75	58	53
5	LEEDS UNITED	42	21	9	12	65	46	51
6	IPSWICH TOWN	42	16	14	12	54	48	46
7	LEICESTER CITY	42	13	19	10	48	51	45
8	MANCHESTER CITY	42	16	11	15	64	46	43
9	TOTTENHAM HOTSPUR	42	14	15	13	63	63	43
10	NORWICH CITY	42	16	10	16	58	58	42
11	EVERTON	42	15	12	15	60	66	42
12	STOKE CITY	42	15	11	16	48	50	41
13	MIDDLESBROUGH	42	15	10	17	46	45	40
14	COVENTRY CITY	42	13	14	15	47	57	40
15	NEWCASTLE UNITED	42	15	9	18	71	62	39
16	ASTON VILLA	42	11	17	14	51	59	39
17	ARSENAL	42	13	10	19	47	53	36
18	WEST HAM UNITED	42	13	10	19	48	71	36
19	BIRMINGHAM CITY	42	13	7	22	57	75	33
20	WOLVERHAMPTON WANDERERS	42	10	10	22	51	68	30
21	BURNLEY	42	9	10	23	43	66	28
22	SHEFFIELD UNITED	42	6	10	26	33	82	22

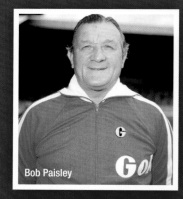

Bob Paisley

Emlyn Hughes

RETRO CHAMPS 1976/77

HOW THE LEAGUE WAS WON

The destiny of the championship had long been in Liverpool's hands and a goalless draw at home to West Ham United on the final Saturday of the league season was enough to see the trophy successfully retained for only the second time in the club's history.

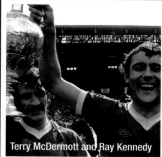

Bob Paisley

Manager: Bob Paisley
Captain: Emlyn Hughes
Top Scorer: **Kevin Keegan (12)**
Most appearances: **Ray Clemence, Emlyn Hughes, Phil Neal (42)**
Number of players used: **17**
Biggest victory: **5-1 v Leicester City (h)**
Heaviest defeat: **1-5 v Aston Villa (a)**
Average attendance: **47,284**

		P	W	D	L	GF	GA	PTS
1	LIVERPOOL	42	23	11	8	62	33	57
2	MANCHESTER CITY	42	21	14	7	60	34	56
3	IPSWICH TOWN	42	22	8	12	66	39	52
4	ASTON VILLA	42	22	7	13	76	50	51
5	NEWCASTLE UNITED	42	18	13	11	64	49	49
6	MANCHESTER UNITED	42	18	11	13	71	62	47
7	WEST BROMWICH ALBION	42	16	13	13	62	56	45
8	ARSENAL	42	16	11	15	64	59	43
9	EVERTON	42	14	14	14	62	64	42
10	LEEDS UNITED	42	15	12	15	48	51	42
11	LEICESTER CITY	42	12	18	12	47	60	42
12	MIDDLESBROUGH	42	14	13	15	40	45	41
13	BIRMINGHAM CITY	42	13	12	17	63	61	38
14	QUEENS PARK RANGERS	42	13	12	17	47	52	38
15	DERBY COUNTY	42	9	19	14	50	55	37
16	NORWICH CITY	42	14	9	19	47	64	37
17	WEST HAM UNITED	42	11	14	17	46	65	36
18	BRISTOL CITY	42	11	13	18	38	48	35
19	COVENTRY CITY	42	10	15	17	48	59	35
20	SUNDERLAND	42	11	12	19	46	54	34
21	STOKE CITY	42	10	14	18	28	51	34
22	TOTTENHAM HOTSPUR	42	12	9	21	48	72	33

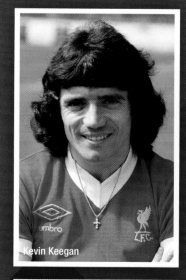

Kevin Keegan

Terry McDermott and Ray Kennedy

15

ALEX
OXLADE-
CHAMBERLAIN

Games	30
Goals	4
Assists	1

ALISSON BECKER

Games	29
Clean Sheets	13
Assists	1

Saturday 11 January 2020 • Venue: Tottenham Hotspur Stadium • Attendance: 61,023 • Referee: Martin Atkinson

TOTTENHAM 0 1 LIVERPOOL

Firmino (37)

MATCH OVERVIEW

Roberto Firmino was the matchwinner as Liverpool marked their first appearance at Tottenham's new stadium by creating history. Victory meant they had taken 61 points from 21 games; a new record across Europe's major top-flight leagues. With Leicester losing earlier in the day, it also extended their lead at the top to 16 points.

THE TEAMS

Tottenham					Liverpool		
	Rose 69'	Son				Alexander-Arnold	
	Sánchez	Winks	Alli	Salah 90'	Oxlade-Chamberlain 61'		Gomez
Gazzaniga				Firmino	Henderson c		Alisson
	Alderweireld c	Eriksen 69'	Moura	Mané 81'	Wijnaldum	van Dijk	
	Tanganga	Aurier				Robertson	

Used subs **Lamela** 69' **Lo Celso** 69'

Used subs **Lallana** 61' **Origi** 81' **Shaqiri** 90'

"There was one team who deserved to win and that was us. That the game was not decided after 50 or 60 minutes was our fault as well. Of course, then it was hectic, very intense. There were a lot of good parts. We should have scored more goals, that's the truth. It was not our best game we played so far, but it was a very good one."

Jürgen Klopp

"They are a good side, a fantastic side. The Champions League final must still hurt for them and they want to bounce back – any chance they have, they will try to beat us. Especially in the second half, they were pressing us and made it very difficult for us. We should have done better but three points is massive, so we're very happy with that."

Virgil van Dijk

Sunday 19 January 2020 • Venue: Anfield • Attendance: 52,916 • Referee: Craig Pawson

LIVERPOOL **2** **0** MAN UTD

van Dijk (14) Salah (90)

MATCH OVERVIEW

A game that Liverpool totally dominated somehow remained in the balance until Mo Salah sealed victory in the final minute. It was the cue for an outpouring of emotion on the pitch and in the stands, with the message from the Kop loud and clear as they chanted 'We're gonna win the League!'

THE TEAMS

Liverpool

Alisson

van Dijk
Gomez
Robertson
Alexander-Arnold

Wijnaldum
Henderson (c)
Oxlade-Chamberlain ⬇ 66'

Mané ⬇ 83'
Firmino ⬇ 83'
Salah

Man Utd

Wan-Bissaka
Lindelöf
Maguire (c)
Shaw ⬇ 87'

Fred
Pereira ⬇ 74'
Matic

James
Martial
Williams ⬇ 74'

de Gea

Used subs **Lallana** 66' ⬆ **Fabinho** 83' ⬆ **Origi** 83' ⬆

Used subs **Greenwood** 74' ⬆ **Mata** 74' ⬆ **Dalot** 87' ⬆

"Big relief! I was really happy with 85 to 90 per cent of the game. It was brilliant. We dominated the game. Everybody should celebrate the situation apart from us. Nothing has changed. We have exactly the same situation, plus three points. It is great, wonderful, unbelievable, but nothing has changed. I will tell you when it feels different. So far, it feels exactly the same."

Jürgen Klopp

"I hadn't scored against United before. I was running fast, I gave Ali my hand and he played it really fast. I was thinking, 'It's the last chance in the game, that ball has to be in.' I wanted to be 100 per cent that I was [putting] the ball in the right spot to score. It was a nice one. I was really excited to score against them."

Mohamed Salah

MATCHDAY TWENTY THREE

Thursday 23 January 2020 • Venue: Molineux • Attendance: 31,746 • Referee: Michael Oliver

WOLVERHAMPTON WANDERERS
Jiminez (51)

1 2

LIVERPOOL
Henderson (8)
Firmino (84)

MATCH OVERVIEW

On a tense night in Wolverhampton, Liverpool's three-month winning streak in the Premier League came perilously close to being curtailed. Thankfully, the team's unrelenting spirit came to the fore again and with six minutes remaining, Roberto Firmino conjured up a winning goal just when it looked as though a point would have to suffice.

THE TEAMS

Wolverhampton Wanderers

Patricio

Saïss
Coady c
Dendoncker

Jonny
Moutinho ⬇ 87'
Neves
Doherty

Jiménez
Neto ⬇ 77'
Traoré

Liverpool

Salah ⬇ 85'
Firmino
Mané ⬇ 33'

Oxlade-Chamberlain ⬇ 70'
Henderson c
Wijnaldum

Alexander-Arnold
Gomez
van Dijk
Robertson

Alisson

Used subs **Jota** 77' ⬆ **Gibbs-White** 87' ⬆

Used subs **Minamino** 33' ⬆ **Fabinho** 70' ⬆ **Origi** 85' ⬆

"We knew before it would be a tough game. They are so different to everything else we face during the year. We don't go for perfection. We go for the perfect reaction so we fight back in difficult situations in the game. That is what the boys did. We won the game which is unbelievable. It was a worldie from Bobby. A super, super goal. I am really, really pleased."

Jürgen Klopp

"[It was an] intense game. We knew it'd be difficult but we knew to keep going, keep fighting. We defended really well, the big man and the back four were brilliant again, the 'keeper. We had some chances as well to put the game to bed. But [we] showed mentality again to keep going and finding that winning goal."

Jordan Henderson

Wednesday 29 January 2020 • Venue: London Stadium • Attendance: 59,959 • Referee: Jonathon Moss

WEST HAM UTD 0 2 LIVERPOOL

Salah (35)

Chamberlain (52)

MATCH OVERVIEW

In what was Liverpool's game in hand over their title rivals, goals either side of half-time in the capital secured a routine win over the struggling Hammers and further increased their lead at the top of the Premier League table to a huge 19 points.

THE TEAMS

WEST HAM UNITED

Masuaku

Cresswell

Lanzini 69'

Noble c

Fabianski Ogbonna

Rice Haller

Diop

Snodgrass

Ngakia

Used subs **Fornals** 69'

LIVERPOOL

Alexander-Arnold 77'

Salah Oxlade-Chamberlain 85'

Gomez

Firmino Henderson c

Alisson

van Dijk

Origi 69' Wijnaldum

Robertson

Used subs **Fabinho** 69' **Keïta** 78' **Jones** 85'

"I'm overly happy with the three points and only one team deserved them. Of course, we could've done things a bit better, but it's not about that. Ali had to make too many saves but honestly who cares! Very often you have to find a way. We didn't quite have the rhythm we wanted...but in the end it's the three points that count."

Jürgen Klopp

"We always said, and we are always saying, we are focused on the next challenge and the next game. The next challenge is the most important of the season. We know our qualities and we know how far we can go but we can only go far if we do big performances on the pitch. The Premier League is top level so you cannot stop and you just need to keep going."

Alisson Becker

HOW THE LEAGUE WAS WON

In what had been a record-breaking season, Liverpool's coronation as champions for an 11th time had long been expected. It was finally confirmed with two games to spare when Aston Villa were beaten 3-0 at Anfield thanks to goals from Kennedy, Dalglish and McDermott.

Liverpool 7 v 0 Tottenham

Manager: Bob Paisley
Captain: Emlyn Hughes/Phil Thompson
Top Scorer: Kenny Dalglish (21)
Most appearances: Ray Clemence, Kenny Dalglish, Ray Kennedy, Phil Neal (42)
Number of players used: 15
Biggest victory: 7-0 v Tottenham Hotspur (h)
Heaviest defeat: 1-3 v Aston Villa (a)
Average attendance: 46,500

		P	W	D	L	GF	GA	PTS
1	LIVERPOOL	42	30	8	4	85	16	68
2	NOTTINGHAM FOREST	42	21	18	3	61	26	60
3	WEST BROMWICH ALBION	42	24	11	7	72	35	59
4	EVERTON	42	17	17	8	52	40	51
5	LEEDS UNITED	42	18	14	10	70	52	50
6	IPSWICH TOWN	42	20	9	13	63	49	49
7	ARSENAL	42	17	14	11	61	48	48
8	ASTON VILLA	42	15	16	11	59	49	46
9	MANCHESTER UNITED	42	15	15	12	60	63	45
10	COVENTRY CITY	42	14	16	12	58	68	44
11	TOTTENHAM HOTSPUR	42	13	15	14	48	61	41
12	MIDDLESBROUGH	42	15	10	17	57	50	40
13	BRISTOL CITY	42	15	10	17	47	51	40
14	SOUTHAMPTON	42	12	16	14	47	53	40
15	MANCHESTER CITY	42	13	13	16	58	56	39
16	NORWICH CITY	42	7	23	12	51	57	37
17	BOLTON WANDERERS	42	12	11	19	54	75	35
18	WOLVERHAMPTON WANDERERS	42	13	8	21	44	68	34
19	DERBY COUNTY	42	10	11	21	44	71	31
20	QUEENS PARK RANGERS	42	6	13	23	45	73	25
21	BIRMINGHAM CITY	42	6	10	26	37	64	22
22	CHELSEA	42	5	10	27	44	92	20

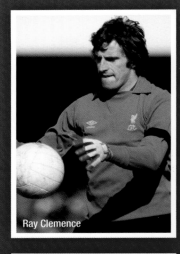

Ray Clemence

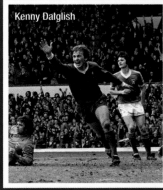

Kenny Dalglish

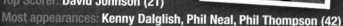

HOW THE LEAGUE WAS WON

The race for the title went down to the final Saturday of the season and for the second successive year Aston Villa were the opponents. If Liverpool slipped up, Manchester United could have capitalised, but they lost at Leeds while David Johnson and Avi Cohen were among the scorers in a 4-1 win at Anfield.

Phil Thompson

Manager: Bob Paisley
Captain: Phil Thompson
Top Scorer: David Johnson (21)
Most appearances: Kenny Dalglish, Phil Neal, Phil Thompson (42)
Number of players used: 17
Biggest victory: 4-0 v Coventry City (h), Bristol City (h), Manchester City (a) & Middlesbrough (h)
Heaviest defeat: 0-2 v Tottenham Hotspur (a)
Average attendance: 44,578

		P	W	D	L	GF	GA	PTS
1	LIVERPOOL	42	25	10	7	81	30	60
2	MANCHESTER UNITED	42	24	10	8	65	35	58
3	IPSWICH TOWN	42	22	9	11	68	39	53
4	ARSENAL	42	18	16	8	52	36	52
5	NOTTINGHAM FOREST	42	20	8	14	63	43	48
6	WOLVERHAMPTON WANDERERS	42	19	9	14	58	47	47
7	ASTON VILLA	42	16	14	12	51	50	46
8	SOUTHAMPTON	42	18	9	15	65	53	45
9	MIDDLESBROUGH	42	16	12	14	50	44	44
10	WEST BROMWICH ALBION	42	11	19	12	54	50	41
11	LEEDS UNITED	42	13	14	15	46	50	40
12	NORWICH CITY	42	13	14	15	58	66	40
13	CRYSTAL PALACE	42	12	16	14	41	50	40
14	TOTTENHAM HOTSPUR	42	15	10	17	52	62	40
15	COVENTRY CITY	42	16	7	19	56	66	39
16	BRIGHTON & HOVE ALBION	42	11	15	16	47	57	37
17	MANCHESTER CITY	42	12	13	17	43	66	37
18	STOKE CITY	42	13	10	19	44	58	36
19	EVERTON	42	9	17	16	43	51	35
20	BRISTOL CITY	42	9	13	20	37	66	31
21	DERBY COUNTY	42	11	8	23	47	67	30
22	BOLTON WANDERERS	42	5	15	22	38	73	25

David Johnson

Liverpool v Aston Villa

12

JOE
GOMEZ

Games	28
Goals	0
Assists	0

FABINHO

Games	28
Goals	2
Assists	3

CHAMPIONS TO CHAMPIONS

1990/91
Manager Kenny Dalglish sensationally resigns mid-season. Graeme Souness replaces him and Liverpool finish runners-up to Arsenal in the First Division.

1991/92
The Reds fall to 8th in the First Division, their lowest placing since 1963, but defeat Sunderland 2-0 at Wembley to win the FA Cup.

1992/93
The Premier League is launched but it's a disappointing campaign for Liverpool who finish sixth.

2001/02
Liverpool finish runners-up to Arsenal in the Premier League and reach the Champions League quarter-final.

2000/01
Houllier's team make history by winning an unprecedented cup treble (League Cup, FA Cup & UEFA Cup) and secure Champions League qualification for the first time.

1999/2000
Although fourth in the league, defeat to Bradford City on the final day of the season sees the Reds narrowly miss out on qualifying for the Champions League again.

2002/03
Manchester United are beaten in the League Cup final but a disappointing campaign in the Premier League sees Liverpool drop three places to fifth.

2003/04
Champions League qualification is secured on the final day of the season but Houllier accepts he's taken Liverpool as far as he can and steps down as manager.

2004/05
With Rafael Benitez now in charge, Liverpool stunningly come back from three goals down to beat AC Milan in the Champions League final in Istanbul.

2013/14
Liverpool look set to be crowned champions for the first time since 1990, but drop vital points towards the end and are overtaken by Manchester City.

2012/13
Brendan Rodgers succeeds Dalglish as manager and Liverpool finish seventh in the Premier League.

2011/12
Liverpool defeat Cardiff City on penalties to win an eighth League Cup. They also reach the FA Cup final but lose to Chelsea.

2014/15
The Reds tumble to a sixth-place finish in the Premier League and are beaten by Aston Villa in the FA Cup semi-final.

2015/16
Jürgen Klopp replaces Rodgers as manager. Liverpool finish eighth in the Premier League and reach two cup finals (League Cup & Europa League) but lose both.

2016/17
More progress is made as Liverpool climb to fourth in the Premier League and clinch Champions League qualification.

A timeline of Liverpool Football Club 1990 to 2020

It's been a long 30-year wait between Liverpool's 18th and 19th league titles but here's a reminder of how the club's fortunes fared during the three decades that spanned these momentous triumphs…

1993/94
Graeme Souness steps down as manager following a 3rd round FA Cup exit to Bristol City. Roy Evans is unveiled as his replacement.

1994/95
Steve McManaman scores twice as Liverpool beat Bolton Wanderers 2-1 at Wembley to lift the League Cup.

1995/96
Liverpool lose 1-0 to Manchester United in a dour FA Cup final at Wembley, but achieve their highest place finish yet in the Premier League: third.

1998/99
After an unsuccessful joint managerial venture, Roy Evans steps down in November leaving Gerard Houllier in charge. Liverpool end the season in seventh place.

1997/98
Liverpool manage to improve their finishing position in the Premier League by one place but it's another trophy-less season at Anfield.

1996/97
Despite topping the table at the turn of the year, Liverpool finish fourth in the Premier League. They reach the semi-final of the European Cup Winners' Cup.

2005/06
West Ham United are beaten on penalties in Cardiff as Liverpool win a seventh FA Cup.

2006/07
It's agony in Athens as Liverpool lose 2-1 to AC Milan in the Champions League final.

2007/08
Despite reaching the last four of the Champions League, it's another disappointing Premier League campaign as Liverpool again fail to mount a serious title challenge.

2010/11
Roy Hodgson replaces Benitez as manager but his tenure lasts only until January when former boss Kenny Dalglish returns to the helm.

2009/10
Liverpool slump to seventh place in the Premier League and fail to progress beyond the Champions League group phase.

2008/09
Liverpool challenge Manchester United strongly in the title race but ultimately have to settle for the runners-up spot, finishing four points behind.

2017/18
Liverpool are beaten finalists in the Champions League, losing 3-1 to Real Madrid in Kiev.

2018/19
Liverpool are crowned champions of Europe for a sixth time. In the Premier League they lose only one game but Manchester City just top them.

2019/20
Runaway leaders Liverpool are finally crowned Premier League CHAMPIONS with a record-breaking seven games to spare.

Saturday 1 February 2020 • Venue: Anfield • Attendance: 53,291 • Referee: Kevin Friend

LIVERPOOL 4 0 SOUTHAMPTON

Chamberlain (47) Salah (72, 90)
Henderson (60)

MATCH OVERVIEW

Four second-half goals in front of the Kop kept the Red machine moving smoothly along the path to Premier League glory, with the gap at the top now increased to a seemingly unassailable 22 points. Never in the history of English top-flight football had there been a bigger margin between the top two teams.

THE TEAMS

Liverpool

Robertson
Wijnaldum ⬇ 81'
van Dijk
Oxlade-Chamberlain ⬇ 73'
Alisson
Fabinho
Firmino
Gomez
Henderson c ⬇ 88'
Salah
Alexander-Arnold

Used subs **Minamino** 81' ⬆ **Keïta** 83' ⬆ **Lallana** 88' ⬆

Southampton

Djenepo Ward-Prowse
Romeu Stephens
Long ⬇ 70'
Højbjerg c Bednarek
Ings ⬇ 70'
McCarthy
Redmond Bertrand

Used subs **Adams** 70' ⬆ **Obafem** 70' ⬆ **Boufal** 82' ⬆

"The attitude and the mentality of these boys made it again possible that we could win this game. Because this was a game which looked in moments not only tricky, it looked like today, yes it will probably happen [Liverpool would drop points]. The boys put a sensational shift in, everybody went to the point and above, so that makes this group really special."

Jürgen Klopp

"Delighted with the performance in the end, especially in the second half. Some really good goals and we've got to be delighted with the three points. We're getting closer to our target but we just need to continue on our journey, keep focussed, keep learning at the training ground and then when we play, give everything we can."

Jordan Henderson

Saturday 15 February 2020 • Venue: Carrow Road • Attendance: 27,110 • Referee: Stuart Atwell

NORWICH CITY 0 1 LIVERPOOL

Mané (78)

MATCH OVERVIEW

Sadio Mané came off the bench and inspired Liverpool to victory over the Premier League's bottom club, netting the only goal of the game 12 minutes from time. With Manchester City not in action until midweek it stretched the lead at the top to 25 points.

THE TEAMS

Norwich City	Liverpool
Byram 27'	Alexander-Arnold
Cantwell	Salah
Hanley (c) McLean	Keïta 84'
	Gomez
Krul	Alisson
Duda Pukki	Firmino Henderson (c)
Zimmermann Tettey 84'	van Dijk
Aarons Rupp 83'	Oxlade-Chamberlain 60' Wijnaldum 60'
	Robertson

Used subs **Lewis** 27' • **Buendia** 83' • **Drmic** 84'

Used subs **Fabinho** 60' • **Mané** 60' • **Milner** 84'

"It was a difficult game for different reasons. The wind, the organisation of the opponent and the way we played first half made it tricky for us. Fabinho coming on was very important for the organisation. Sadio was fresh and he helped us to win the game. The gap is so insane; I don't really understand it. I'm not smart enough. I've not had that before. It's outstanding."

Jürgen Klopp

"We are doing very well. We still have more games, [it's] one step. We are Liverpool. We are a strong team and the boys do a great job. We're happy with our result today. We will do everything possible as a team and carry on in the same way. We'll see what's going to happen at the end of the season."

Sadio Mané

Monday 24 February 2020 • Venue: Anfield • Attendance: 53,313 • Referee: Jonathon Moss

LIVERPOOL **3** **2** WEST HAM UTD

Wijnaldum (9) Mané (81)	Diop (12)
Salah (68)	Fornals (54)

MATCH OVERVIEW

On a nervy night at Anfield, West Ham almost pulled off a shock result before Liverpool fought back to preserve their long-unbeaten record. In a five-goal thriller it required a late Sadio Mané winner to eventually seal a record-equalling 18th straight Premier League victory, leaving them just four more wins away from the title.

THE TEAMS

Liverpool

Robertson
van Dijk (c)
Wijnaldum
Alisson
Fabinho
Gomez
Keïta 57'
Alexander-Arnold

West Ham United

Mané 90'
Firmino
Salah
Antonio
Noble (c)
Anderson 65'
Snodgrass 84'
Rice
Soucek 47'
Ngakia
Diop
Ogbonna
Fabianski
Cresswell

Used subs **Oxlade-Chamberlain** 57' **Matip** 90'

Used subs **Fornals** 47' **Haller** 65' **Bowen** 84'

"Could I have wished for a better position to go into these last 11 games? No, I would never have thought it was possible, but each one of them is really difficult. We just have to be ready for the hardest work. We were tonight as a unit, together with the crowd again and I really love that fact, I couldn't appreciate it more, it's really special."

Jürgen Klopp

"We felt like we dominated the game but it's football and we've let them have two chances. The fans were unbelievable, they were massively with us, especially when we were behind or conceded a goal, so for us it's a massive help to have the fans like that. We just tried to keep going and it paid off in the end."

Trent Alexander-Arnold

Saturday 29 February 2020 • Venue: Vicarage Road • Attendance: 21,634 • Referee: Michael Oliver

WATFORD 3 0 LIVERPOOL

Sarr (54, 60)
Deeney (72)

MATCH OVERVIEW

All good things must come to an end and, on an evening to forget in Hertfordshire, an unusually lacklustre Liverpool conceded three second-half goals in 18 minutes as their remarkable run of 27 Premier League games without defeat since the start of the season was brought to a crashing halt.

THE TEAMS

WATFORD

Foster

Cathcart **c**   Capoue

Kabasele   Hughes

Masina

Femenia

Deulofeu ⬇ 37'

Doucouré ⬇ 89'   Deeney

Sarr ⬇ 82'

LIVERPOOL

Alexander-Arnold

Salah   Oxlade-Chamberlain ⬇ 65'

Firmino ⬇ 79'   Fabinho   Lovren

Mané   van Dijk **c**

Wijnaldum ⬇ 61'

Robertson

Alisson

Used subs Pereyra 37' ⬆ Pussetto 82' ⬆ Chalobah 89' ⬆

Used subs Lallana 61' ⬆ Origi 65' ⬆ Minamino 79' ⬆

"We were not good enough, simple as that. Watford did exactly what they wanted to do, we didn't do exactly what we should have done. The game was not clicking right today… Congratulations. Really well done and well deserved."

Jürgen Klopp

"Losing hurts. Credit to Watford. They deserved it. The records are only for the media, we didn't even mention it once… We want to strike back, we want to show what we've been doing the whole season. That's the only way forward."

Virgil van Dijk

"To beat possibly the best club side in the world at the moment - well, not possibly, they are, is testament to how we played. So, it's very satisfying."

Nigel Pearson
(Watford manager)

HOW THE LEAGUE WAS WON

After plummeting to 12th place in the table on Boxing Day, Liverpool produced a stunning run of form that meant victory over Tottenham in their penultimate game would secure the title. At half-time they trailed 1-0 but goals from Lawrenson, Dalglish and Whelan saw them crowned champions for a 13th time.

Manager: **Bob Paisley**
Captain: **Phil Thompson/Graeme Souness**
Top Scorer: **Ian Rush (17)**
Most appearances: **Bruce Grobbelaar, Kenny Dalglish, Phil Neal (42)**
Number of players used: **16**
Biggest victory: **5-0 v Manchester City (a)**
Heaviest defeat: **1-3 v Manchester City (h)**
Average attendance: **35,213**

		P	W	D	L	GF	GA	PTS
1	LIVERPOOL	42	26	9	7	80	32	87
2	IPSWICH TOWN	42	26	5	11	75	53	83
3	MANCHESTER UNITED	42	22	12	8	59	29	78
4	TOTTENHAM HOTSPUR	42	20	11	11	67	48	71
5	ARSENAL	42	20	11	11	48	37	71
6	SWANSEA CITY	42	21	6	15	58	51	69
7	SOUTHAMPTON	42	19	9	14	72	67	66
8	EVERTON	42	17	13	12	56	50	64
9	WEST HAM UNITED	42	14	16	12	66	57	58
10	MANCHESTER CITY	42	15	13	14	49	50	58
11	ASTON VILLA	42	15	12	15	55	53	57
12	NOTTINGHAM FOREST	42	15	12	15	42	48	57
13	BRIGHTON & HOVE ALBION	42	13	13	16	43	52	52
14	COVENTRY CITY	42	13	11	18	56	62	50
15	NOTTS COUNTY	42	13	8	21	61	69	47
16	BIRMINGHAM CITY	42	10	14	18	53	61	44
17	WEST BROMWICH ALBION	42	11	11	20	46	57	44
18	STOKE CITY	42	12	8	22	44	63	44
19	SUNDERLAND	42	11	11	20	38	58	44
20	LEEDS UNITED	42	10	12	20	39	61	42
21	WOLVERHAMPTON WANDERERS	42	10	10	22	32	63	40
22	MIDDLESBROUGH	42	8	15	19	34	52	39

Alan Hansen

HOW THE LEAGUE WAS WON

Bob Paisley's sixth and last league title as manager was a foregone conclusion from early in the season; so much so that Liverpool failed to win any of their final seven games and still finished 11 points clear. The title was confirmed by results elsewhere following a 2-0 defeat at Tottenham.

Bob Paisley

Manager: **Bob Paisley**
Captain: **Graeme Souness**
Top Scorer: **Ian Rush (24)**
Most appearances: **Bruce Grobbelaar, Kenny Dalglish, Alan Kennedy, Phil Neal (42)**
Number of players used: **16**
Biggest victory: **5-0 v Southampton (h) & Everton (a)**
Heaviest defeat: **1-3 v West Ham United (a)**
Average attendance: **34,836**

		P	W	D	L	GF	GA	PTS
1	LIVERPOOL	42	24	10	8	87	37	82
2	WATFORD	42	22	5	15	74	57	71
3	MANCHESTER UNITED	42	19	13	10	56	38	70
4	TOTTENHAM HOTSPUR	42	20	9	13	65	50	69
5	NOTTINGHAM FOREST	42	20	9	13	62	50	69
6	ASTON VILLA	42	21	5	16	62	50	68
7	EVERTON	42	18	10	14	66	48	64
8	WEST HAM UNITED	42	20	4	18	68	62	64
9	IPSWICH TOWN	42	15	13	14	64	50	58
10	ARSENAL	42	16	10	16	58	56	58
11	WEST BROMWICH ALBION	42	15	12	15	51	49	57
12	SOUTHAMPTON	42	15	12	15	54	58	57
13	STOKE CITY	42	16	9	17	53	64	57
14	NORWICH CITY	42	14	12	16	52	58	54
15	NOTTS COUNTY	42	15	7	20	55	71	52
16	SUNDERLAND	42	12	14	16	48	61	50
17	BIRMINGHAM CITY	42	12	14	16	40	55	50
18	LUTON TOWN	42	12	13	17	65	84	49
19	COVENTRY CITY	42	13	9	20	48	59	48
20	MANCHESTER CITY	42	13	8	21	47	70	47
21	SWANSEA CITY	42	10	11	21	51	69	41
22	BRIGHTON & HOVE ALBION	42	9	13	20	38	68	40

Ian Rush

27

DIVOCK
ORIGI

Games	28
Goals	4
Assists	1

JAMES
MILNER

Games	22
Goals	2
Assists	2

7

Saturday 7 March 2020 • Venue: Anfield • Attendance: 53,323 • Referee: Paul Tierney

LIVERPOOL 2 1 BOURNEMOUTH

Salah (25)
Mané (33)

Wilson (9)

MATCH OVERVIEW

The Reds bounced back from the shock of their first league defeat to chalk up a record 22nd consecutive home win. Despite falling behind early, two goals in eight minutes by Mo Salah and Sadio Mané eased any nerves and moved Liverpool to within nine points of the title.

THE TEAMS

Liverpool	Bournemouth
Milner c	Fraser Stacey
Wijnaldum	Billing S. Cook c ⬇19'
van Dijk	
Adrián Fabinho Mané	Wilson Lerma ⬇80' Ramsdale
Gomez Firmino ⬇90'	L. Cook Aké
Oxlade-Chamberlain Salah	
Alexander-Arnold ⬇84'	Stanislas ⬇68' Smith

Used subs **Lallana** 84' ⬆ **Origi** 90' ⬆

Used subs **Simpson** 19' ⬆ **Solanke** 68' ⬆ **Gosling** 80' ⬆

"I was absolutely happy about the result, the three points and the performance because I knew it would be tricky for different reasons. We wanted to fight back before the game and how we played after being 1-0 down was exceptional, to be honest. The boys' reaction today, I loved - I really loved."

Jürgen Klopp

"The confidence of everyone was a bit down but today we showed the winning mentality is back. The team came back after the early goal from Bournemouth; we showed again that we are here to face the end of the season and face the big challenges that are coming. The three points was the most important thing today, and we got them."

Adrián San Miguel

Sunday 21 June 2020 • Venue: Goodison Park • Attendance: N/A • Referee: Mike Dean

EVERTON 0 0 LIVERPOOL

MATCH OVERVIEW

Football's suspension due to the Covid-19 pandemic had put everything into perspective but after a 15-week hiatus, Liverpool resumed their quest for the title with a stalemate at Goodison. Water breaks, extra substitutes and no fans; it all felt a bit different. The prize at stake remained the same though and the Reds were edging ever closer to it.

THE TEAMS

Everton

Pickford

Digne
Holgate
Keane
Coleman c

Gordon 60'
Gomes
Davies
Iwobi 88'

Richarlison
Calvert-Lewin 90'

Minamino 45'
Firmino 65'
Mané 65'

Henderson c
Fabinho
Keïta 65'

Alexander-Arnold
Matip 73'
van Dijk
Milner 43'

Alisson

Liverpool

Used subs **Sigurdsson** 60' **Iwobi** 88' **Kean** 90'

Used subs **Gomez** 43' **Oxlade-Chamberlain** 45' **Origi** 65' **Wijnaldum** 65' **Lovren** 73'

"It was a real fight. Both teams showed that they understand it's a derby - even without a crowd. It was intense, physical, all-in. We didn't have a lot of chances. Most of the time we were dominant but they had the biggest chance - that's how it is. It came out of the blue. We were lucky in that moment but apart from that, we were in control."

Jürgen Klopp

"Obviously everyone didn't know really what to expect, the whole procedure before the game and how things will go, and it was just good to be back out. Obviously, we wanted to win, we wanted to get the three points, but we're another step closer. We'll try to improve every time and we'll see how that will develop over the next couple of weeks."

Virgil van Dijk

Wednesday 24 June 2020 • Venue: Anfield • Attendance: N/A • Referee: Martin Atkinson

LIVERPOOL 4 0 CRYSTAL PALACE

Alexander-Arnold (23) Fabinho (55)
Salah (44) Mané (69)

MATCH OVERVIEW

An all-round outstanding team performance swept Palace aside and left Liverpool on the brink of finally ending their 30-year wait for a 19th league title. At an eerily empty Anfield, the ruthless Reds scored four goals without reply and the much-coveted trophy was now within touching distance.

THE TEAMS

Robertson ⬇84'
van Dijk
Alisson
Gomez
Alexander-Arnold ⬇74'

Wijnaldum
Fabinho
Henderson c ⬇64'

Mané ⬇84'
Firmino ⬇74'
Salah

Ayew ⬇84'

Townsend
Kouyaté ⬇66'
McArthur ⬇66'
McCarthy
Zaha ⬇15'

Ward
Cahill c
Hennessey
Sakho
Van Aanholt

Used subs Oxlaide-Chamberlain 64' ⬆ Williams 74' ⬆
Minamino 74' ⬆ Elliott 84' ⬆ Keïta 84' ⬆

Used subs Meyer 15' ⬆ Milivojevic 66' ⬆ Riedewald 66' ⬆
Pierrick 84' ⬆

"Wow. Imagine if this stadium would have been full today, and all the people would have experienced it live. It would have been amazing. The boys played like everyone was in the stadium. They pushed themselves and the atmosphere on the pitch was incredible. Today was for sure the best counter-pressing game I saw behind closed doors! I liked it a lot. Wonderful result, wonderful game."

Jürgen Klopp

"I think we put in a world-class performance, probably one of our best of the season, so it's something to be proud of. We've come here after such a long time and obviously without the fans it was difficult. It was different but we put in a performance to be proud of."

Trent Alexander-Arnold

Thursday 2 July 2020 • Venue: Etihad Stadium • Attendance: N/A • Referee: Anthony Taylor

MAN CITY 4 0 LIVERPOOL

De Bruyne (25) Foden (45)
Sterling (35) Oxlade-Chamberlain OG (66)

MATCH OVERVIEW

In the grand scheme of the title race this result was immaterial. City's defeat at Chelsea a week earlier had seen Liverpool confirmed as the 2019/20 Premier League champions without playing. The long-time leaders came out to a guard of honour but then failed to take their chances and paid the price.

THE TEAMS

Man City

Ederson

Walker 73'
Garcia
Laporte 79'
Mendy

Rodrigo
Gündogan

De Bruyne c
Foden
Sterling 79'

Jesus 58'

Liverpool

Alisson

Alexander-Arnold
Gomez 45'
van Dijk
Robertson 76'

Henderson c
Fabinho
Wijnaldum 62'

Salah
Firmino 62'
Mané 85'

Used subs **Mahrez** 58' **Cancelo** 73' **Otamendi** 79'
B.Silva 79'

Used subs **Oxlade-Chamberlain** 45' **Origi** 62' **Keïta** 62'
Williams 76' **Minamino** 85'

"We didn't behave like somebody who became champions a week ago. We lacked fluidity. And in some 50-50 situations they were quicker than us. We had probably more chances than we had in games which we won, but we didn't use them."

Jürgen Klopp

"We are not making any excuses. We are bitterly disappointed. On another night I'd like to think we can finish our chances and it would change the game but unfortunately it wasn't to be and you've got to give credit to City."

Jordan Henderson

"We beat the champions, an extraordinary team. We are brave to play, they are brave to play. My team I like every single game. We tried to play football, take risks. The best team I have ever faced in my life."

Pep Guardiola (Manchester City manager)

RETRO CHAMPS 1983/84

HOW THE LEAGUE WAS WON

Meadow Lane, home of Notts County, was the setting as a third successive league title was clinched. A goalless draw against the already-relegated hosts provided the point needed in the penultimate league game of the season to confirm Liverpool as champions for a 15th time.

Manager: Joe Fagan
Captain: Graeme Souness
Top Scorer: Ian Rush (32)
Most appearances: Bruce Grobbelaar, Alan Hansen, Alan Kennedy, Mark Lawrenson, Sammy Lee (42)
Number of players used: 15
Biggest victory: 6-0 v Luton Town (h) & West Ham United (h)
Heaviest defeat: 0-4 v Coventry City (a)
Average attendance: 32,021

		P	W	D	L	GF	GA	PTS
1	LIVERPOOL	42	22	14	6	73	32	80
2	SOUTHAMPTON	42	22	11	9	66	38	77
3	NOTTINGHAM FOREST	42	22	8	12	76	45	74
4	MANCHESTER UNITED	42	20	14	8	71	41	74
5	QUEENS PARK RANGERS	42	22	7	13	67	37	73
6	ARSENAL	42	18	9	15	74	60	63
7	EVERTON	42	16	14	12	44	42	62
8	TOTTENHAM HOTSPUR	42	17	10	15	64	65	61
9	WEST HAM UNITED	42	17	9	16	60	55	60
10	ASTON VILLA	42	17	9	16	59	61	60
11	WATFORD	42	16	9	17	68	77	57
12	IPSWICH TOWN	42	15	8	19	55	57	53
13	SUNDERLAND	42	13	13	16	42	53	52
14	NORWICH CITY	42	12	15	15	48	49	51
15	LEICESTER CITY	42	13	12	17	65	68	51
16	LUTON TOWN	42	14	9	19	53	66	51
17	WEST BROMWICH ALBION	42	14	9	19	48	62	51
18	STOKE CITY	42	13	11	18	44	63	50
19	COVENTRY CITY	42	13	11	18	57	77	50
20	BIRMINGHAM CITY	42	12	12	18	39	50	48
21	NOTTS COUNTY	42	10	11	21	50	72	41
22	WOLVERHAMPTON WANDERERS	42	6	11	25	27	80	29

Graeme Souness

Phil Neal

RETRO CHAMPS 1985/86

HOW THE LEAGUE WAS WON

On the final Saturday of the league campaign, Kenny Dalglish scored the goal that secured the club's 16th First Division title at the expense of Merseyside rivals Everton. It was his first year as player/manager and it came against Chelsea at Stamford Bridge in front of 10,000 travelling Liverpool supporters.

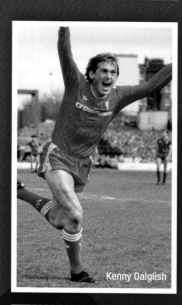
Alan Hansen

Manager: Kenny Dalglish
Captain: Alan Hansen
Top Scorer: Ian Rush (22)
Most appearances: Bruce Grobbelaar (42)
Number of players used: 18
Biggest victory: 6-0 v Oxford United (h)
Heaviest defeat: 0-2 v Arsenal (a) & Everton (h)
Average attendance: 35,316

		P	W	D	L	GF	GA	PTS
1	LIVERPOOL	42	26	10	6	89	37	88
2	EVERTON	42	26	8	8	87	41	86
3	WEST HAM UNITED	42	26	6	10	74	40	84
4	MANCHESTER UNITED	42	22	10	10	70	36	76
5	SHEFFIELD WEDNESDAY	42	21	10	11	63	54	73
6	CHELSEA	42	20	11	11	57	56	71
7	ARSENAL	42	20	9	13	49	47	69
8	NOTTINGHAM FOREST	42	19	11	12	69	53	68
9	LUTON TOWN	42	18	12	12	61	44	66
10	TOTTENHAM HOTSPUR	42	19	8	15	74	52	65
11	NEWCASTLE UNITED	42	17	12	13	67	72	63
12	WATFORD	42	16	11	15	69	62	59
13	QUEENS PARK RANGERS	42	15	7	20	53	64	52
14	SOUTHAMPTON	42	12	10	20	51	62	46
15	MANCHESTER CITY	42	11	12	19	43	57	45
16	ASTON VILLA	42	10	14	18	51	67	44
17	COVENTRY CITY	42	11	10	21	48	71	43
18	OXFORD UNITED	42	10	12	20	62	80	42
19	LEICESTER CITY	42	10	12	20	54	76	42
20	IPSWICH TOWN	42	11	8	23	32	55	41
21	BIRMINGHAM CITY	42	8	5	29	30	73	29
22	WEST BROMWICH ALBION	42	4	12	26	35	89	24

Kenny Dalglish

8
NABY
KEÏTA

Games	18
Goals	2
Assists	3

20
ADAM
LALLANA

Games	15
Goals	1
Assists	1

ADRIÁN

Games	11
Clean Sheets	2
Assists	0

DEJAN
LOVREN

6

Games	10
Goals	0
Assists	1

Sunday 5 July 2020 • Venue: Anfield • Attendance: N/A • Referee: Paul Tierney

LIVERPOOL 2 0 ASTON VILLA

Mané (71)
Jones (90)

MATCH OVERVIEW

On their first return to Anfield since being crowned champions Liverpool got back to winning ways and preserved their unbeaten home record in the league. Sadio Mané broke the deadlock midway through the second-half, while young Curtis Jones came off the bench late in the game to grab his first Premier League goal and seal the points.

THE TEAMS

Liverpool

Robertson 90'
van Dijk c
Keïta 85'
Alisson
Fabinho 61'
Gomez
Oxlaide-Chamberlain 61'
Alexander-Arnold
Mané
Origi 61'
Salah

Aston Villa

El Ghazi 74'
Konsa
Luiz
Hause
Davis 74'
Grealish c
Reina
McGinn
Mings
Trézéguet 85'
Taylor

Used subs **Firmino** 61' **Henderson** 61' **Wijanaldum** 61' **Jones** 84' **Williams** 90'

Used subs **Jota** 74' **Samatta** 74' **Vassilev** 85'

"It was a very difficult game, for different reasons. Aston Villa were well-organised and made it really tricky for us. We made three changes in decisive areas, which was important I think from a physical point of view. We are where we are because we win the difficult games, and that happened again tonight."

Jürgen Klopp

"I'm just grateful for the manager and the rest of the staff for having the belief in me and putting me out there when it was only 1-0 and Villa were playing well. He said just to try and get a hold of the game by the scruff of the neck and control the game a bit more. That's what I tried to do and hopefully the goal helped."

Curtis Jones

Wednesday 8 July 2020 • Venue: Amex Stadium • Attendance: N/A • Referee: Craig Pawson

BRIGHTON & HOVE ALBION
Trossard (45)

1   **3**

LIVERPOOL
Salah (6, 76)
Henderson (8)

MATCH OVERVIEW

Liverpool became the fastest English club in history to reach the landmark figure of 30 league wins in a season (34 games). Mo Salah netted twice, set up Jordan Henderson's goal and went close to a hat-trick. The only downside to the night being an injury sustained by the captain.

THE TEAMS

Brighton					Liverpool		
	Burn					Alexander-Arnold	
	Mac Allister ⬇ 71'			Salah		Keïta ⬇ 61'	
Dunk c		Trossard					Gomez
Ryan	Stephens	Groß ⬇ 71'		Firmino	Henderson c		Alisson
	Webster	Maupay		⬇ 87'	80'	van Dijk	
	Pröpper ⬇ 71'		Oxlade-Chamberlain	Wijnaldum		
	Lamptey			⬇ 61'		Williams ⬇ 45'	

Used subs **Bissouma** 71' ⬆ **Connolly** 71' ⬆ **Mooy** 90' ⬆

Used subs **Robertson** 45' ⬆ **Fabinho** 61' ⬆ **Mané** 61' ⬆ **Milner** 80' ⬆ **Minamino** 87' ⬆

"It was a difficult game against a good opponent, a deserved win. Job done, job well done in big parts of the game but not in all. That's how it is. I think we started really, really well, we finished really, really well, but in between we left the door a bit too wide open for Brighton."

Jürgen Klopp

"I think it was a good game for fans to watch. We were lucky a bit to score in the beginning twice, but they played a good game. After 2-1 they had more confidence and were close to scoring a second as well, so after I scored the third one it made the game calm again."

Mohamed Salah

Saturday 11 July 2020 • Venue: Anfield • Attendance: N/A • Referee: David Coote

LIVERPOOL 1 1 BURNLEY

Robertson (34)   Rodriguez (69)

MATCH OVERVIEW

An inspired performance by Clarets' keeper Nick Pope ultimately denied Liverpool victory and brought the champions' one hundred per cent home record to an end. Despite dominating for most of the game, Pope's heroics restricted the Reds to just one goal – a rare Andy Robertson header – and their failure to add a second proved costly when Rodriguez later equalised.

THE TEAMS

Liverpool

Alisson

van Dijk c
Gomez
Williams 69'

Jones 69'
Fabinho
Wijnaldum 81'

Robertson 90'

Mané
Origi
Salah

Burnley

Wood 65'
Rodriguez

Pieters 65'   Bardsley
Westwood   Long
Brownhill   Tarkowski c
McNeil   Taylor

Pope

Used subs **Alexander-Arnold** 69' ⬆ **Keïta** 69' ⬆
Oxlade-Chamberlain 81' ⬆

Used subs **Gudmundsson** 65' ⬆ **Vydra** 65' ⬆

"It was a good performance in most parts of the game. There were moments when it was Liverpool against Nick Pope. It's hard to create against a team so organised but we created super chances. I'm fine for the performance for 80 minutes and it was probably one of our best games against Burnley, but we couldn't get a second and that's why we've been left with a point."

Jürgen Klopp

"We hit the bar late on but I think three points would have been over-egging it. We defended well and our keeper played well. They're a fine side, they're all over you so quickly and we couldn't get a foothold in the first half."

Sean Dyche (Burnley manager)

Wednesday 15 July 2020 • Venue: Emirates Stadium • Attendance: N/A • Referee: Paul Tierney

ARSENAL 2 1 LIVERPOOL

Lacazette (32)
Nelson (44)

Mané (20)

MATCH OVERVIEW

Despite taking the lead through Sadio Mané and looking to be in complete control of the game, uncharacteristic defensive errors by Virgil van Dijk and Alisson Becker gifted Arsenal two goals before the break and they were enough to consign Liverpool to just a third league defeat of the season.

THE TEAMS

Sako 85'
Tierney
Xhaka
Martínez   Luiz
Torreira 57'
Holding
Cédric 76'

Pépé
Lacazette c 57'
Nelson 58'

Alexander-Arnold
Salah
Oxlade-Chamberlain 61'
Firmino 61'
Gomez
Fabinho
van Dijk c
Alisson
Mané
Wijnaldum 83'
Robertson

Used subs Ceballos 57' ▲ Willock 57' ▲ Aubameyang 58' ▲
Maitland-Niles 76' ▲ Kolasinac 85' ▲

Used subs Keïta 61' ▲ Minamino 61' ▲ Origi 83' ▲
Shaqiri 83' ▲

"We took a break at 1-0. Twice a massive lack of concentration and these two moments killed the game for us. Arsenal had no real chances, but you cannot win football games when you concede goals like this. We have to learn from that 100%, and we will. Tonight we got punished."

Jürgen Klopp

"We dominated and put pressure on them but gave them two goals, obviously it's then difficult to come back. If you give goals away like we did today you get what you deserve… until then nothing was wrong. We pressed them and scored a fantastic goal. I made a mistake, I take the blame for it, I take it as a man, and we move on."

Virgil van Dijk

RETRO CHAMPS 1987/88

HOW THE LEAGUE WAS WON

Spearheaded by a trio of exciting new signings, Liverpool blazed a trail across the First Division. They topped the table from November and were never in danger of relinquishing their place. The coronation of the long-time champions-elect came five games from the end when Peter Beardsley scored in a 1-0 home win over Tottenham.

Peter Beardsley

Manager: Kenny Dalglish
Captain: Alan Hansen
Top Scorer: John Aldridge (26)
Most appearances: Steve Nicol, Steve McMahon (40)
Number of players used: 22
Biggest victory: 5-0 v Nottingham Forest (h)
Heaviest defeat: 1-2 v Nottingham Forest (a)
Average attendance: 39,682

		P	W	D	L	GF	GA	PTS
1	LIVERPOOL	40	26	12	2	87	24	90
2	MANCHESTER UNITED	40	23	12	5	71	38	81
3	NOTTINGHAM FOREST	40	20	13	7	67	39	73
4	EVERTON	40	19	13	8	53	27	70
5	QUEENS PARK RANGERS	40	19	10	11	48	38	67
6	ARSENAL	40	18	12	10	58	39	66
7	WIMBLEDON	40	14	15	11	58	47	57
8	NEWCASTLE UNITED	40	14	14	12	55	53	56
9	LUTON TOWN	40	14	11	15	57	58	53
10	COVENTRY CITY	40	13	14	13	46	53	53
11	SHEFFIELD WEDNESDAY	40	15	8	17	52	66	53
12	SOUTHAMPTON	40	12	14	14	49	53	50
13	TOTTENHAM HOTSPUR	40	12	11	17	38	48	47
14	NORWICH CITY	40	12	9	19	40	52	45
15	DERBY COUNTY	40	10	13	17	35	45	43
16	WEST HAM UNITED	40	9	15	16	40	52	42
17	CHARLTON ATHLETIC	40	9	15	16	38	52	42
18	CHELSEA	40	9	15	16	50	68	42
19	PORTSMOUTH	40	7	14	19	36	66	35
20	WATFORD	40	7	11	22	27	51	32
21	OXFORD UNITED	40	6	13	21	44	80	31

John Barnes

John Aldridge

RETRO CHAMPS 1989/90

HOW THE LEAGUE WAS WON

Title number 18 was confirmed following a 2-1 victory at home to Queens Park Rangers in the third to last game of the season. That result in itself would not have been enough but news then came through that Aston Villa had only drawn with Norwich, meaning the Reds could no longer be overtaken at the top.

Manager: **Kenny Dalglish**
Captain: **Alan Hansen**
Top Scorer: **John Barnes (22)**
Most appearances: **Bruce Grobbelaar, Steve McMahon (38)**
Number of players used: **21**
Biggest victory: **9-0 v Crystal Palace (h)**
Heaviest defeat: **1-4 v Southampton (a)**
Average attendance: **36,873**

		P	W	D	L	GF	GA	PTS
1	**LIVERPOOL**	38	23	10	5	78	37	79
2	ASTON VILLA	38	21	7	10	57	38	70
3	TOTTENHAM HOTSPUR	38	19	6	13	59	47	63
4	ARSENAL	38	18	8	12	54	38	62
5	CHELSEA	38	16	12	10	58	50	60
6	EVERTON	38	17	8	13	57	46	59
7	SOUTHAMPTON	38	15	10	13	71	63	55
8	WIMBLEDON	38	13	16	9	47	40	55
9	NOTTINGHAM FOREST	38	15	9	14	55	47	54
10	NORWICH CITY	38	13	14	11	44	42	53
11	QUEENS PARK RANGERS	38	13	11	14	45	44	50
12	COVENTRY CITY	38	14	7	17	39	59	49
13	MANCHESTER UNITED	38	13	9	16	46	47	48
14	MANCHESTER CITY	38	12	12	14	43	52	48
15	CRYSTAL PALACE	38	13	9	16	42	66	48
16	DERBY COUNTY	38	13	7	18	43	40	46
17	LUTON TOWN	38	10	13	15	43	57	43
18	SHEFFIELD WEDNESDAY	38	11	10	17	35	51	43
19	CHARLTON ATHLETIC	38	7	9	22	31	57	30
20	MILLWALL	38	5	11	22	39	65	26

Kenny Dalglish

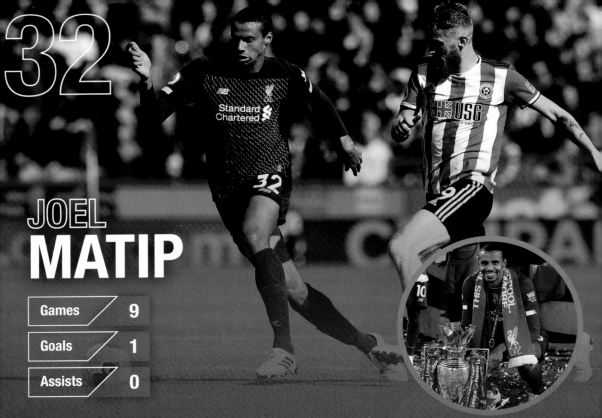

32

JOEL
MATIP

Games	9
Goals	1
Assists	0

23

XHERDAN
SHAQIRI

Games	7
Goals	1
Assists	0

18

TAKUMI
MINAMINO

Games	10
Goals	0
Assists	0

76

NECO
WILLIAMS

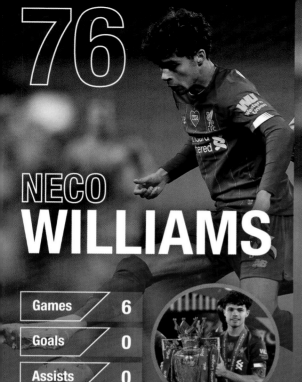

Games	6
Goals	0
Assists	0

67

HARVEY
ELLIOTT

Games	2
Goals	0
Assists	0

48

CURTIS
JONES

Games	6
Goals	1
Assists	0

Wednesday 22 July 2020 • Venue: Anfield • Attendance: N/A • Referee: Andre Marriner

LIVERPOOL 5 3 CHELSEA

Keïta (23)　　　Firmino (55)　　　　　　　Giroud (45)　　Pulisic (73)
Alexander-Arnold (38)　Oxlade-Chamberlain (84)　　Abraham (61)
Wijnaldum (43)

MATCH OVERVIEW

On the night Jordan Henderson received the Premier League trophy from Sir Kenny Dalglish, Liverpool celebrated in style with victory in an eight-goal thriller. They raced into a three-nil lead inside 43 minutes, but Chelsea fought back and the points were never truly safe until Oxlade-Chamberlain sealed the win six minutes from time.

THE TEAMS

Liverpool

Robertson

van Dijk Ⓒ

Alisson

Gomez

Alexander-Arnold

Wijnaldum ▼ 66'　Mané ▼ 87'

Fabinho　Firmino ▼ 87'

Keïta ▼ 66'　Salah ▼ 79'

Chelsea

James

Willian ▼ 59'　Azpilicueta Ⓒ

Jorginho

Giroud ▼ 59'　Zouma　Arrizabalaga

Kovacic

Mount ▼ 59'　Rüdiger

Alonso ▼ 88'

Used subs **Jones** 66' ▲ **Milner** 66' ▲ **Oxlade-Chamberlain** 79' ▲ **Minamino** 87' ▲ **Origi** 87' ▲

Used subs **Abraham** 59' ▲ **Hudson-Odoi** 59' ▲ **Pulisic** 59' ▲ **Emerson** 88' ▲

"Tonight it was very difficult because Chelsea was so good so I couldn't be more proud of the boys, throwing in a performance like this in an open game. Nice goals. Incredible goals. Super football in moments. I loved the game so we could enjoy the rest of the night. Now we have a party, then we have to recover."

Jürgen Klopp

"We knew what we needed to do, we knew what was coming afterwards, but the job in hand was to make sure we got three points today. I'm glad that we did it. Credit to them, they had moments in the game but we managed to keep going and find a few more goals in the end. It put a nice little cherry on a really nice night for us."

Alex Oxlade-Chamberlain

Sunday 26 July 2020 • Venue: St James' Park • Attendance: N/A • Referee: Anthony Taylor

NEWCASTLE UTD 1 3 LIVERPOOL

Gayle (1)

van Dijk (38) Mané (89)
Origi (59)

MATCH OVERVIEW

Liverpool signed off an unforgettable season in impressive fashion by coming from behind to register their 32nd league win of the campaign. The champions recovered from the shock of conceding within 26 seconds and eventually ran out deserved winners – a result that saw them reach the 99-point mark; a new club record.

THE TEAMS

Ritchie

Rose 74'

Almirón 70'

Saint-Maximim 45'

Oxlade-Chamberlain 64'

Keïta 86'

Williams 85'

Gomez

Dubravka Fernández Bentaleb 49'

Gayle 70'

Origi 64'

Wijnaldum

van Dijk

Alisson

Manquillo Shelvey Ⓒ

Minamino 64'

Milner Ⓒ

Robertson

Lazaro

Used subs **Joelinton** 45' **Longstaff** 49' **Carroll** 70'
Hayden 70' **Watts** 74'

Used subs **Firmino** 64' **Mané** 64' **Salah** 64'
Alexander-Arnold 85' **Jones** 86'

"Our target for the day was to finish on a high and we did it. We needed a little wake-up call and from that moment on the boys worked really hard to play against this defensive wall of Newcastle. It was not perfect, but like our season, the boys don't only win games on the perfect days, they are ready to really dig deep on the not-so-perfect days."

Jürgen Klopp

"We all wanted to play today, we all want to show why we are the champions, we wanted to win the game. We knew it was going to be tough and I think we made it even more difficult for ourselves [after] I don't know how many seconds! But we played well, second half especially we played amazing football. It's good to finish off the season on a high."

Virgil van Dijk

A huge outpouring of emotion greeted the confirmation that Liverpool Football Club was back on its perch as champions of England for the first time in 30 years. Here's how members of the first team squad and a selection of club legends reacted to the news....

"Winning and being champion is always something special, but being Premier League champion for the first time in the history of this club means a lot for us. I believe we put our names in the history of this club. We are part of something big here."

Alisson Becker

"We are Premier League champions and we are proud of that. It's something we've always dreamed of. As fans I think it's something that will always be remembered."

Trent Alexander-Arnold

"It's been a dream come true for all of us. It's something I always hoped for when I joined Liverpool. It's just amazing. Everyone has to feel like a champion who is part of us, including the fans of course."

Virgil van Dijk

"I'm really happy that this time we can give this title to the supporters because they have waited so long for this. That makes it more beautiful because when you have such loyal supporters and you can give them one of the best gifts, it makes it more beautiful than it is."

Gini Wijnaldum

"It's a special moment and a unique moment. It has been a long [time] waiting for the title and finally we got it and you can see how happy the players, the staff, the manager, [the people] around the club, all over the world the supporters are."

Sadio Mané

"To win the Premier League, it's unbelievable. I can't describe with words. When I came here, I said I wanted to win the Premier League. For the city it is something else. Everybody is crazy about the result, everybody is crazy about the Premier League."

Mo Salah

"We knew everyone was desperate for this. It's been great for us to enjoy it as players but think how long the fans have waited. Younger generations had only seen it on videos or online. Driving around the city, seeing all the flags outside houses, I know how much it means."

James Milner

"We may not have realized the importance yet, but I think we will always be remembered. The way we won it, with the huge points difference between us and second place, is really something to celebrate."

Fabinho

"I think the emotion of this one is probably greater, although I've not been involved in it, than the ones I was involved in. Because fortunately we won it quite regularly, not every year but nearly every year. So, you never get fed up with winning, but to win it for the first time in over 30 years, even for the fans, for them, you see the enjoyment and the pleasure in their faces they've had through the victory. I think that would probably be a little bit better than when we won it."

Sir Kenny Dalglish (LFC player 1977-90 & manager 1985-91 & 2011-12)

"This is for the younger generation of Liverpool supporters. They have had to grow up on stories from their parents and grandparents of what it's like for Liverpool to win the title and now they get to experience it themselves. It's fantastic."

Ian Rush (LFC player 1980-87 & 88-96)

"It's great to be champions again and may it continue! It's great for Liverpool fans and people like myself who have been associated with the club for so long and not seen that Premier League title."

Roy Evans
(LFC manager 1994-98)

"I think it's been nothing short of miraculous…a marvellous achievement from a marvellous manager and a great squad of players. They deserve everything that they have got. It has been coming."

Gary Gillespie (LFC player 1983-91)

"From the first Friday night at Anfield against Norwich, they have simply blown the opposition apart. A remarkable season that will live long in the memories of everybody."

Jan Molby (LFC player 1984-95)

"Congratulations to Liverpool on winning the Premier League. Incredible achievement from a fantastic squad of top players. Lead by a world class manager and coaching team; also a special mention for the backing from FSG. And lastly and most importantly the fans who have waited 30 years. Let the party begin."

Steven Gerrard (LFC player 1998-2015)

"For me, this is amazing for the supporters, for the players and for the so many people working inside Liverpool. So many people work there and for the last 30 years they didn't know how it felt for Liverpool to win the Premier League. For the Liverpool supporters, for the club, for the Scouse people. I am so happy for them."

Luis Suarez
(LFC player 2011-14)

"Huge congrats to everyone at Liverpool Football Club on winning the Premier League. Unbelievable squad, magnificent manager, great staff but above all my sincere congrats to every single LFC supporter. You've been waiting so long and finally that desired trophy is yours. Very well deserved. YNWA."

Fernando Torres (LFC player 2007-11)

LIVERPOOL FC
2019/20 PREMIER LEAGUE
RESULTS & STATS

RESULTS

Date		Opponent	Score		Date		Opponent	Score
Aug 09	(H)	Norwich City	4-1		Jan 02	(H)	Sheffield United	2-0
Aug 17	(A)	Southampton	2-1		Jan 11	(A)	Tottenham Hotspur	1-0
Aug 24	(H)	Arsenal	3-1		Jan 19	(H)	Manchester United	2-0
Aug 31	(A)	Burnley	3-0		Jan 23	(A)	Wolverhampton Wanderers	2-1
Sep 05	(H)	Newcastle United	3-1		Jan 29	(A)	West Ham United	2-0
Sep 22	(A)	Chelsea	2-1		Feb 01	(H)	Southampton	4-0
Sep 28	(A)	Sheffield United	1-0		Feb 15	(A)	Norwich City	1-0
Oct 05	(H)	Leicester City	2-1		Feb 24	(H)	West Ham United	3-2
Oct 20	(A)	Manchester United	1-1		Feb 29	(A)	Watford	0-3
Oct 27	(H)	Tottenham Hotspur	2-1		Mar 07	(H)	Bournemouth	2-1
Nov 02	(A)	Aston Villa	2-1		Jun 21	(A)	Everton	0-0
Nov 10	(H)	Manchester City	3-1		Jun 24	(H)	Crystal Palace	4-0
Nov 23	(A)	Crystal Palace	2-1		Jul 02	(A)	Manchester City	0-4
Nov 30	(H)	Brighton & Hove Albion	2-1		Jul 05	(H)	Aston Villa	2-0
Dec 04	(H)	Everton	5-2		Jul 08	(A)	Brighton & Hove Albion	3-1
Dec 07	(A)	Bournemouth	3-0		Jul 11	(H)	Burnley	1-1
Dec 14	(H)	Watford	2-0		Jul 15	(A)	Arsenal	1-2
Dec 26	(A)	Leicester City	4-0		Jul 22	(H)	Chelsea	5-3
Dec 29	(H)	Wolverhampton Wanderers	1-0		Jul 26	(A)	Newcastle United	3-1

APPEARANCES

Roberto Firmino	38
Virgil van Dijk	38
Trent Alexander-Arnold	38
Georginio Wijnaldum	37
Andy Robertson	36
Sadio Mané	35
Mohamed Salah	34
Jordan Henderson	30
Alex Oxlade-Chamberlain	30
Fabinho Tavarez	28
Alisson Becker	29
Joe Gomez	28
Divock Origi	28
James Milner	22
Naby Keïta	18
Adam Lallana	15
Adrian San Miguel	11
Dejan Lovren	10
Takumi Minamino	10
Joel Matip	9
Xherdan Shaqiri	7
Curtis Jones	6
Neco Williams	6
Harvey Elliott	2

GOALSCORERS

Mohamed Salah	19
Sadio Mané	18
Roberto Firmino	9
Virgil van Dijk	5
Jordan Henderson	4
Alex Oxlade-Chamberlain	4
Divock Origi	4
Georginio Wijnaldum	4
Trent Alexander-Arnold	4
Naby Keïta	2
James Milner	2
Andy Robertson	2
Fabinho Tavarez	2
Joel Matip	1
Curtis Jones	1
Adam Lallana	1
Xherdan Shaqiri	1
Own Goals	2

ASSISTS

Trent Alexander-Arnold	13
Andy Robertson	12
Mohamed Salah	10
Roberto Firmino	8
Sadio Mané	7
Jordan Henderson	5
Fabinho Tavarez	3
Naby Keïta	3
James Milner	2
Divock Origi	1
Virgil van Dijk	1
Adam Lallana	1
Alisson Becker	1
Dejan Lovren	1
Alex Oxlade-Chamberlain	1

LEAGUE TABLE

			P	W	D	L	GF	GA	PTS
1		LIVERPOOL	38	32	3	3	85	33	99
2		MANCHESTER CITY	38	26	3	9	102	35	81
3		MANCHESTER UNITED	38	18	12	8	66	36	66
4		CHELSEA	38	20	6	12	69	54	66
5		LEICESTER CITY	38	18	8	12	67	41	62
6		TOTTENHAM HOTSPUR	38	16	11	11	61	47	59
7		WOLVERHAMPTON WANDERERS	38	15	14	9	51	40	59
8		ARSENAL	38	14	14	10	56	48	56
9		SHEFFIELD UNITED	38	14	12	12	39	39	54
10		BURNLEY	38	15	9	14	43	50	54
11		SOUTHAMPTON	38	15	7	16	51	60	52
12		EVERTON	38	13	10	15	44	56	49
13		NEWCASTLE UNITED	38	11	11	16	38	58	44
14		CRYSTAL PALACE	38	11	10	17	31	50	43
15		BRIGHTON & HOVE ALBION	38	9	14	15	39	54	41
16		WEST HAM UNITED	38	10	9	19	49	62	39
17		ASTON VILLA	38	9	8	21	41	67	35
18		BOURNEMOUTH	38	9	7	22	40	65	34
19		WATFORD	38	8	10	20	36	64	34
20		NORWICH CITY	38	5	6	27	26	75	21

ALEX
RAISBECK

DONALD
MACKINLAY

RON
YEATS

TOMMY
SMITH

GRAEME
SOUNESS

HI